ALL THAT
THIS
HOUSE
HAS TO
OFFER

ALL THAT THIS HOUSE HAS TO OFFER

A STORY COLLECTION

BETTY R WALL

atmosphere press

Published by Atmosphere Press

Cover design by Kevin Stone

Atmospherepress.com

In memory of my parents,
Jacob and Katie Wall

Author's Note

These stories are rooted in family. Some might call them "heritage stories." There are those inspired by my own lived experiences and memories thereof, and others that are inspired by the stories told by my parents and grandmothers. Where memory fails, or where there are gaps in oft-told stories, the creative mind takes over.

I have tried to capture the sentiment of the times in 1943, as my parents were fleeing Ukraine, and the lives they created for themselves in Austria and later for us in Canada. It is a remarkable journey.

For the sake of storytelling, I have created scenes around historical events. Any historical inaccuracies presented in the stories are entirely my own.

CONTENTS

The truth about stories is that that's all we are.

– Thomas King

FEAST DAY

It was one of those summer mornings in the 1960s. I lay in bed, drifting in and out of sleep, trying to remember what day it was. The cool morning air flowed in through the open window. The rooster crowed. A gunshot. I bolted upright, threw the covers off my bed, drew back the curtains. The sun was just creeping toward Mt. Baker, its light already showing off the perpetually snow-capped mountain. The air was still.

And then I remembered. It was feast day! The pig. I saw Dad coming from the direction of the pigpen with a rifle in his hand, and Mr. Paquet, our hired hand, close behind. I sometimes had nightmares of Dad missing the pig and hitting Mr. Paquet instead, but there he was, Mr. Paquet, walking tall and straight, a few steps behind Dad. He stopped to blot his pants with a handkerchief. Blood spatters, likely. Mr. Paquet always wore off-white pants, crisp and clean, the pleats pressed neatly. A beige French worker's cap completed his outfit.

I opened my bedroom door and breathed in the smell of freshly brewed coffee. I loved the smell of coffee with its promises of a new day, fresh baking, laughter, and conversation. If only it tasted as good as it smelled. I walked into the kitchen, wiping the sleep from my eyes. Dirty breakfast dishes on the table, jam jars open with spoons stuck in them, bits of butter left in the butter dish, one lone bun in the bread basket, half-empty coffee cups.

"It's about time you got up," Mom said. "*Gut geschlafen?*"

I looked at the clock. It was eight o'clock in the morning. "The gunshot woke me," I said.

"Yeah, that always makes me jump as well," she said. "I'm always relieved when I see your Dad and Mr. Paquet coming out of the pen."

"Why does Dad ask Mr. Paquet to stand beside the pig?" I asked. "I would never do that."

"It's so the pig doesn't move," she said.

"Yeah, but what if Dad missed? Poor Mr. Paquet!"

"He's never missed," Mom said calmly. "Papa is a good shot." She spooned yeast into a small Mason jar, added sugar and warm water, stirred it with a spoon, and set it on top of the stove. I loved watching the yeast come alive, the spongy texture rising slowly to the top. I inhaled its yeasty smell, the promise of beautiful loaves of bread at the end of a long, hard day.

"White bread?" I asked.

"*Ja*," she said.

I hovered over the stove. An empty stainless steel stockpot sat on the largest element. "Is this for *Borscht*?"

"*Ja*," Mom said. "Have some breakfast. The *Omas* will be here any minute and then it's time to get to work."

"Okay." I grabbed the remaining bun from the bread basket, pulled it apart, and slathered it with cherry jam. I could really smell the yeast working now.

A car door slammed. Then another. I jumped up from the kitchen table and went to the back door. When I stepped out onto the carport, I saw Oma Wall—her bright white hair pulled back into a bun, deep blue eyes peering from behind her gold-rimmed glasses and heard her booming voice. With her cane in one hand, she grabbed the railing with the other and pulled herself up the stairs. Oma Sawatzky followed. A slight woman, a soft step, and a quiet voice, her grey-green eyes all lined and crinkly and warm, grey hair pulled back into a bun.

"*Mensch*, it's a beautiful day," Oma Wall said. "*Na, wie geht's?*" she said, pinching my cheeks.

"*Gut*," I said and gave her a big hug. I stooped in turn to hug Oma Sawatzky.

"Where do you want us to start?" Oma Sawatzky asked Mom quietly, taking off her coat. She pulled a yellow oil-cloth apron out of her handbag, pulled it over her head, and tied it behind her. Oma Wall did the same; hers was blue and white. Out came the white cotton kerchiefs, made from flour sacks. Each tied theirs under their chin.

Mom had her hands deep in the bread-mixing bowl. Mixing, kneading, and slapping the dough until it was soft and smooth. She opened a bottle of vegetable oil, poured a teaspoon into her hand, and smoothed it over the dough. Then she took the Tupperware cover, laid it on top of the bowl, and ran her thumbs around the rim until it snapped shut. She set the bowl on top of the warm stove for the dough to proof.

"There," she said, wiping her hands on her apron. "That's done for a bit. Let's head outside to the shed."

I quickly pulled on my cut-off jeans and a T-shirt and followed them. Outside, a cast iron cauldron filled three-quarters full of water sat on top of an open fire, steaming. While we were getting ready in the kitchen, the men had killed a dozen or so chickens. One or two still flopped around on the ground, not quite ready to let go. The severed heads were piled in a bucket, their glassy eyes looking up at me.

"Gather them up!" Oma Wall called out to me. I did as I was told, skirting around the ones still flopping about.

Oma Sawatzky grabbed a hen from me and plunged it into the steaming cauldron, then placed it on her lap and began plucking. Her small hands grabbed big clumps of feathers and dropped them onto the ground. Occasionally, a damp feather got caught under her plain gold wedding band and she paused to slide it out. Once the bulk of the feathers was removed, she set the hen aside.

"Here," she said. "With your young eyes, you'll see what I've missed. Make sure you get all the fine feathers I couldn't see."

I picked the hen up and plucked the remaining coarse feathers here and there, marvelling at the strength of the quills attached to them. I gave the almost-naked birds the once-over and set them aside. Once each hen was plucked and re-plucked, Mom grabbed them one by one and held them gently over the fire, singeing any remaining downy bits and then dropping them into a clean laundry basket.

While we women plucked and prepared the chickens, the men primed the pig. I wandered past the shed, over to where they worked. The pig lay on the ground, a large pool of blood gathered where its neck had been slit.

"It has to bleed out," Dad always told me. "You have to remove as much blood as possible, otherwise, bacteria begins to grow. It destroys the meat." Dad stood there holding a large knife. The sharpening rod hung on his belt.

"You sure you want to see this?" he asked when he saw me.

"Yup," I said. "I've seen it before, but I find it fascinating."

"It looks as though the bleeding has stopped," Dad said. "Time to scald and scrape. Kind of like plucking chickens."

"But we can't plunge a whole pig into the cauldron," I said.

"No, no, we need buckets of scalding hot water to pour

over the carcass, and then we'll begin scraping. There are mostly bristles on the skin, so we won't have to pluck like with the chickens. Just scrape to get the skin smooth. First, we'll have to get the pig up off the ground and onto this pallet. John? Grab the front legs and I'll grab the back." On the count of three, they hoisted the carcass onto the pallet.

"There's another cauldron of hot water just over at the shed. Want to help us carry buckets of hot water over here?" Dad asked, looking at me.

"Sure," I said hesitantly, worried that the scalding water would land on my bare legs. I grabbed an aluminum milk pail and ran over to the shed, dipped it into the scalding water, and walked back to the pig as quickly as I could, holding the pail away from me. Dad poured the water over the pig and started scraping at one end of the carcass while John scraped at the other. I kept coming with pails of hot water. Once they met in the middle of the carcass, they rolled it over and continued on the other side.

Dad ran his hand over the skin, and once assured that it was clean and smooth, gave it a satisfying pat.

"Okay," he said, "that looks good. How about we just give it one more rinse? B, can you get us another pail of water?"

I grabbed the pail again and off I went. The Omas were nattering away in the shed, still plucking chickens. The laundry basket was almost overflowing with naked hens.

"They've got you running, haven't they?" Oma Wall said.

"Yeah. One more pail full and the pig will be clean. Almost as clean as these chickens," I said, laughing.

"Go on, then," Oma said. "I'm sure they're waiting for you."

I walked as quickly as the scalding water allowed and set the bucket beside the pig. John grabbed it and slowly poured it over the now-cleaned and scraped carcass. I ran my hand over it. The skin felt thick and smooth. I ran my hand over my own skin. So thin in comparison.

Dad and John pulled the pallet toward a monkey bar that my brothers sometimes used to do pull-ups. A pulley system was rigged up to the bar. Dad grabbed a steel bar with pointed ends and hooked it through the hind legs of the pig, just above the feet. A pull-chain with a hook slid through the centre of the bar to hoist the carcass. Dad slowly pulled on the chain, hoisting up the pig, while John held onto the bar to steady it.

Once the pig was taut and secure, Dad gathered up his other tools for evisceration. "Just hold it on one side so it doesn't swing." John moved to one side and stepped up onto a small platform so he could steady himself and the pig.

Dad took the knife and made an incision around the left hock. With a crack, the foot was severed. He moved to the right hock and repeated the swift motion. Then the head. He cut behind each ear, then moved to the joint at the back of the skull. With a swift motion and a crack, the head fell. I stood there, mesmerized.

"You still okay?" Dad asked.

"*Ja*," I said.

"Hold it there, John," Dad said. John stood there on the small wooden step, his entire body leaning against the pig, holding it in a tight embrace. Dad wiped the knife on his white butcher's apron, swiped it six times on the sharpening stone, and tested it gingerly with his left index finger.

"Perfect," he said. With great precision and care, he slit the skin at the front end and deftly made his way down one side and then the other. Soon it lay in a heap on the ground, still slightly attached to its owner. Dad gave the skin a tug and, with a sudden motion, pulled it right off the carcass.

"You know pig skin is used to make footballs, right?" he said.

"Really?" I said.

Again, Dad wiped the knife and reached for the sharpening steel. I watched as he drew the knife across the steel—scrape scrape, scrape scrape, scrape scrape—there was a rhythm to it. Six times across.

Then he cut right down the centre of the pig, from top to bottom, and pulled the entrails out of the steaming body, from esophagus to anus, in one fell swoop. It smelled. I gagged. There were the organs—the heart, the lungs, and the steaming stomach. Yuck, gross, fascinating.

"They say our organs are very similar to that of the pig," Dad said. I looked at the heart, so red and vibrant, the distended stomach. Knees bent, he lifted it and carried it off to one side. "We've got to get the stomach cleaned quickly. Can you bring the hose a bit closer?" I ran over to the little egg shed and pulled on the green garden hose. "Now, turn the water on, but not too much." I ran back to the tap and turned it ever so slightly. "A little more," he said. I continued turning until he held up his hand, then stopped. I ran back over to him. "Now, you hold the hose here," he said, pointing to one end of the intestine, probably the esophagus, "and just let the water run." I stood there with the hose as he palpated the stomach. It got bigger and bigger until it looked like a beach ball. Then he took a small knife out of his pocket and slit the bottom of the stomach. The steaming contents poured out. Bits of corn and watermelon rind—I had fed him those last night. "Keep the hose going, so we get it nice and clean."

"What do we use the stomach for?" I asked.

"We don't really use the stomach, but we'll use the intestines to make casings for sausages," he said, pulling the intestines out from the stomach. There were yards of them. Soon they lay in a neat coil in a white enamel bowl.

"Wow!" I said.

"We will get a lot of sausages out of these," he said, chuckling and whooping. "Now take those over to your mom and the Omas for proper cleaning, okay?"

I grabbed the bowl of slippery insides and walked over to the egg shed, where the Omas were waiting.

"Let me see," Oma Wall said. She grabbed one end of the intestines and pulled them through her fingers. "*Sehr schön.*" Lovely. She took a big pot of very hot water and vinegar and poured it into a bowl. Then she started washing the intestines as if she was washing delicates, gathering them up and swishing them through the water, squeezing gently. Every time she squeezed, her plain gold wedding band caught the light coming in through the window.

From the shed, we could hear the men talking. They were close enough so I could hear their tones, but not close enough to make out what they were saying. I wondered what they were discussing. I always loved hanging around, listening. I never said anything. I knew that sometimes they talked about the old country—back in Russia. How many times had we heard "When I was twelve, I had to be the man of the house. When we were kids, we were grateful to get an apple for Christmas. An apple—can you imagine? Nothing ever tasted so sweet." We got bored with it. The church was always a good topic, as was farming, of course. Egg quotas, chicken quotas, berry yields, but never money. That topic was taboo. Wives? I don't think so. Kids? Then I heard "...animals...food...give thanks...everything...purpose..." The voices were getting louder.

"What are you daydreaming about?" Oma Wall asked, giving me a slight nudge.

"Oh, just thinking," I said.

"C'mon, get back to work," she said.

Oma Sawatzky sat there quietly. She had started scraping the intestines very gently so as not to puncture them.

I often wondered why they never spoke about my *Opas,* their husbands. They were arrested during the war in Russia. Oh, we had heard that story over and over again, about the hardships and Oma Sawatzky, the quiet one, going off to prison to try to see her husband, watching as the prisoners were led down the street and then quietly crossing the street so that her husband could catch a glimpse of her. She never told that story. It was my mom and my Aunt Irene who told the stories and kept them alive. My cousins and I used to imagine what it would be like if one or the other of our grandfathers suddenly appeared, having somehow miraculously escaped Russia. We heard these stories from time to time, how one husband had been sent to the labour camps in Siberia and managed to get out, arriving in Canada twenty years later to find that his wife had remarried, assuming he was never coming back. My Omas never remarried. I wondered if they had other admirers. I think they just held out hope that their men would return one day. They never spoke of it.

"How about a story, Oma?" I said, looking at Oma Sawatzky.

"Now?"

"*Ja.* What better time? Something from your childhood."

She looked at me over the top of her glasses and grinned.

"Okay. So, there was a boy in our village who wanted to become a preacher. Whenever an animal died, he asked us—girls mostly—to gather 'round for the burial and to play the part of the mourners. He played the part of the preacher, of course, held a Bible high in front of him, and said 'Oh death, where is thy victory? Where is thy sting?' He was so serious. We just could not contain ourselves. We laughed and laughed until the tears ran down our cheeks. Oh, he got so angry with us. 'This is serious,' he'd say, and lash out at us. We laughed even harder. And then, later in life, when he actually became a preacher, I could never listen to him without thinking of those funeral ceremonies he put us through," she said, laughing and shaking her head.

"Your turn, Oma," I said, looking at Oma Wall. "Do you have any stories? Like how you met my Opa?"

"What? Why are you askin' me that now? Get to work," she said.

"Just curious," I said.

"While Oma Sawatzky finishes up with the intestines, let's start on the chickens," she said.

"I thought we were done with those."

"We're done with the outer cleaning, and now we need to eviscerate them. I'll show you how," she said. "Let's take them up to the house where we've got more room to work."

I grabbed the laundry basket full of chickens and started toward the main house, staggering under the weight of it. Oma Wall grabbed her cane and followed closely behind.

"I'll come as soon as I'm finished with these," Oma Sawatzky said.

Oma Wall and I walked past the steel swing set Dad and Mr. Danielson—the foul-mouthed super skilled mechanic from down the road—had built for us, past the old pear tree and the well, through the garage and into the basement. Mom had cleared a big surface for us on which to work. I set the laundry basket on top of a big stool. Oma Wall grabbed a knife from the knife block. It had a wider blade at the top, which gradually tapered to a point.

"Your Papa must have done a lot of butchering with this knife," she said. "Look how worn it is."

"Oh, is that why it looks so funny?" I asked. "I always wondered why it was that shape. I've never seen a knife like that in the store."

"Hand me one of those," she said, her left hand outstretched.

I grabbed a chicken by the legs and handed it to her.

"So, first we cut off this bit here." She pointed the knife to the end of the chicken's butt and cut swiftly into one side, then the other. With a twist, she broke off the pope's nose and tossed it into the garbage can. Then she turned the chicken around and pulled at the neck until it stretched and created a vacuum. In went her hand, grabbing at something. She tugged until she got what she was after and out came a small bulbous sack. "This is the crop," she said. "Feel it." I took it from her and poked at it. "It must have eaten just before it was killed. That's all grain in there."

"It feels kind of neat," I said, palpating it with my fingers.

"That goes in the garbage too," she said. "Next, we open up the cavity." She took a knife and slit the bird just above the butt. Setting the knife aside, she reached into the bird and, in one fell swoop, pulled out the organs. She tugged carefully at the liver and set it aside. Then she grabbed a bit that contained something green.

"Be really careful not to cut into this," she said. "This

is the bile duct. If any of this spills into the cavity of the bird, we won't be able to eat it." She removed it swiftly and threw it into the garbage pail. Back in went her hand and out came the heart. I loved the heart. It was my favourite offal. Then the gizzard.

"Look at this," she said. She tapped it with her knife, slit it down the middle, and opened it up. Inside were tiny pebbles and feed, partly masticated. "Now, we just pull this piece of tough skin right off the gizzard and discard it. Once the gizzard has been cleaned thoroughly, we can bake it right along with the rest of the chicken."

"I like the gizzard, actually," I said. "It's a bit chewy, but I like that."

Oma glanced at me quickly above the rim of her glasses and grinned.

Next, she grabbed a pair of scissors, cut off the neck, and tossed it aside. "Go ask your mom for some vinegar. We will fill the laundry tub with vinegar and water and wash the hens until the water is clear."

I ran up the basement stairs and opened the door to the kitchen. The smell of bread baking was intoxicating. I inhaled deeply.

"What do you need?" Mom asked.

"Vinegar."

Mom grabbed the bottle of white vinegar and handed it to me.

"The bread smells soooo good," I said, peering through the glass oven door.

"It's almost done," Mom said.

"Are you coming?" Oma Wall shouted from the basement.

"*Ja, ja!*" I said. "Gotta go, Mom."

When I got back to the eviscerating table, Oma Wall

pulled out an egg, completely formed, encased in a membrane, the hard shell not yet formed. "*Schau* mal," she said, "*ein Windei*." A wind egg. "Here, put your hand in here. I think there might be another one." I placed my hand into the warm cavity of the chicken and pulled out a completely formed egg, again without the hard shell. It was perfect.

"Have you ever seen a little tiny chick in one of those eggs?" I asked.

"Now that would be something," she said. "We've only got hens here, no eggs have been fertilized."

"I hear the roosters crowing sometimes," I said. "We try really hard to separate the roosters from the hens because we need the eggs."

"Hmmmm."

I looked at her, hair pulled back in a severe bun, her hands moving swiftly as she worked.

"So, how did you meet my Opa?"

"This again," she said with a chuckle. "Well, we both sang in the church choir. And one day, he asked if he could walk me home."

"Oh—how old were you?" I asked.

"Eighteen," she said. "We got married when I was nineteen."

"That's just a few years older than I am now. How did you know he was the one?"

"I just did," she said.

"Do you think about him sometimes?"

She stopped for a second to look at me. "There is no point. Sometimes I dream about him. I don't like to think about what happened to him."

"But Oma, some men have come back from Siberia," I said. "Maybe Opa will come back."

"*Ach*, you are a dreamer. Those few men who returned and made it to Canada, they are like strangers to their families."

"Do you have anything special of his that you were able to keep?"

She looked at her thin gold wedding band. "My wedding ring," she said, "six children, and twenty-three grandchildren! And one worn and tattered photograph. I am blessed. *Der liebe Gott hat uns behütet.* The good Lord protected us."

"What did he look like, my Opa? What was he like?"

"He wasn't a big man. About as tall as your father."

"Was he good-looking?"

"Your father looks like him," she said. "He had dark hair."

"And his name was Jacob too, wasn't it?" I asked.

"*Ja.* That is how we did things then. The first son was named after the father and the first daughter after the mother."

"But why does Dad have another J in his name? He always says his name is Jacob Jacob. Why have two names the same?" I asked.

"In Russia, it was customary to do that. It was really to show that he was the son of Jacob," she said.

"Do you miss him?"

She stopped, knife in mid-air. "Like I said, I dream about him sometimes. Not in a while though. But every night when I go to bed, and I pray for the safety of my family, I think of him too."

"I wish I could have met him," I said. "Oma?"

She looked at me.

"Do you think I'll ever meet anyone?" I asked.

"Any boy would be lucky to be with you," she said.

"Really?" I grinned.

"Look at you. Young and pretty, bright blue eyes, a gorgeous smile," she said.

"Yeah, but Dad keeps telling me I'm fat and my brothers keep telling me only the fat boys will like me and want to go out with me," I said. "Dad never makes those kinds of comments to the guys. Not fair."

She laughed her bright, guttural belly laugh. "Your Papa loves you very much," she said.

Suddenly, Dad burst into the basement. "Okay," he said, "we're ready for you outside."

It was non-stop work apart from a little lunch break. Food wolfed down as quickly as possible and back outside. It was hot. Throughout the afternoon, we made sausages, ribs, and cracklings, my Omas taking turns stirring the cauldron. I ran from station to station, taking orders from everyone.

By late afternoon, Mom was back in the kitchen, adding the last bit of seasoning to the big pot of *Borscht*. My mouth watered.

"Could you get me some plums?" Mom asked. "Just go pick them off the tree. There's probably quite a few on the ground as well. They'll be just perfect for a nice plum *plautz*."

"Plum *plautz!* My absolute favourite!" I grabbed a bowl and ran into the garden. Almost everything had been harvested by this time. There was just the odd ear of corn, some potatoes, and carrots left. Peas and beans, cucumbers, and all the berries had been harvested, frozen, canned, or pickled.

I gathered up the plums on the ground first, stopping to pop one and then another into my mouth. Oh, they were so sweet, just on the edge of too sweet, the flavour intoxicating. I filled the bowl with a few from the tree and ran back into the house.

"It's about time," Mom said. "What were you doing out there? Daydreaming?"

I laughed. "No, just testing the fruit," I said, as if she couldn't see my plum-stained lips.

"Wash and chop them for me, okay? Everyone will be in for dinner soon. And once you've got that done, set the table."

"Okay. Does that mean I don't have to collect eggs today?" I asked, hoping that was the case. Man, it was unfair. I had to do everything. Work in the house, work in the barn, serve at the table, run when Dad and the boys asked me to.

"I'll tell your brothers they have to do your chores today," she said, smiling at me.

I grinned from ear to ear as I opened up the kitchen cupboard and took out the old china. Over the years, Mom had collected the light grey dishes with little rose petals on the rim from the Esso station. We had a whole set. Dinner plates, lunch plates, soup bowls, cups and saucers, bread plates. I set everything out, remembering knives, forks, spoons, and Dad's special silver soup spoon he had brought from Russia. It had to be washed with great care. No S.O.S. pads or Dutch Cleanser ever touched the surface of that spoon. Only soap and hot water. I looked at it for some time before I put it next to his knife.

By six o'clock, the men had come in from outdoors. They washed and scrubbed in the basement before coming into the kitchen. The Omas removed their aprons, washed their hands, and wet, combed, and pinned back the strands of hair that had come undone during the day. Dad sat at the head of the table, as always. He looked tired and hungry.

Once everyone was seated, Dad bowed his head in prayer. "Vater segne diese Speise, uns zur Kraft und Dir zum Preise. Amen."

"Amen," we murmured in unison.

Dad opened his eyes and rubbed his hands together in anticipation. Mom brought the steaming pot of *Borscht* to the table and set it down. Huge farmer-sized slices of bread sat in baskets, begging to be eaten. Dad filled his bowl first then waited impatiently while the rest of us filled ours.

"*Guten Appetit*," he said. We raised our spoons and dug in. There was silence apart from cutlery clanking against bowls and plates and the occasional "Pass the bread, pass the butter."

"I'm glad we got that done today," Dad said. "It's supposed to rain tomorrow."

It was hard to imagine, given the day we had had. Brilliant sunshine, a perfect day.

I cleared the bowls from the table and brought out the plum *plautz*—"pie by the yard," to our English-speaking friends. Plump, juicy plum bits covered with a crumb topping, browned just so. Mom cut the slices, plum juice oozing out, still warm. I could hardly wait to sink my teeth into it. The sweetness of the plums and the slight tartness of it all. My definition of heaven.

"Thank you," Dad said after dinner. He pushed back from the table and went back outside. He was heading out for a smoke. A bit of quiet for him at the end of a long, exhausting, yet satisfying day.

JACOB
AND KATIE

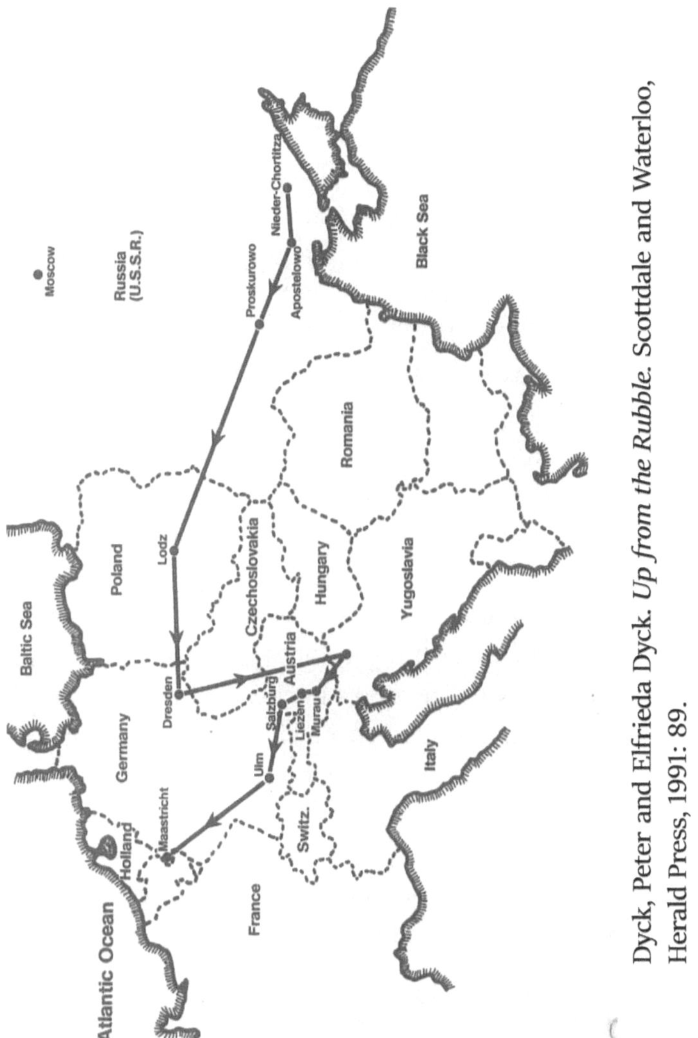

Dyck, Peter and Elfrieda Dyck. *Up from the Rubble.* Scottdale and Waterloo, Herald Press, 1991: 89.

The journey in the "Jacob and Katie" story takes us as far as Austria. On September 5, 1948, the group with which they had been in Austria in various refugee camps was then shipped to Bremen, Germany, and two weeks later to Cuxhafen where they took the SS Samaria to Quebec.

"Tell me that story again," I said, taking Mom's hand in mine, her worn gold wedding band glinting in the afternoon sun.

"Which story is that?"

"You know, the one where you tell Oma Wall that you're going to the village marketplace and that, along with a few groceries, you're going to bring Jacob home. Home from the war. It just sounds so romantic to me. So impossible and so wonderful!"

She smiled coyly, pursing her lips. It was a hot summer day in the late 1980s. She was wearing a Hawaiian muu-muu, splashed with big purple and white hibiscus flowers, and rested her tanned legs on a kitchen chair. We sat at the kitchen table, custom-made from cherry wood, handcrafted by Mr. Bartsch, Dad's best friend. The sliding glass door was open, letting in a warm, gentle breeze. Jars filled with luscious, dark sour cherry jam lined the kitchen counter. Just then, one of them popped to signal it was sealed. We looked at one another and grinned.

"How many is that now?" she asked.

"Four. Don't worry, I'm counting."

"Well, it was October 1945," she said. "My mother, my two brothers, and I were living in a rundown house in St. Peter am Kammersberg, a peaceful little village nestled in the mountains of Austria. The Austrians were so welcoming, which was such a relief after three years on the run, just escaping the firebombing at Dresden and then raids by partisans in what was then Yugoslavia." She paused and reflected. "Anyway, it was a Saturday morning. I remember that because it was market day."

"And where was Dad?"

"We didn't know exactly. He was in the German army. His mother got mail from time to time and the last we heard, he had been taken prisoner of war by the British and was in Belgium. Some of the other young men from our village had returned, but not Jacob. Oma Wall was really worried."

"How did he even end up in the German army?"

"He turned eighteen in February 1944 when we were in Yugoslavia and that's when he was conscripted. What a crazy time that was," she said, shaking her head. "Off he went to training camp. As Mennonites, we were against the war, but it didn't matter. He had to go and so did all the other young men."

"How did you end up in Yugoslavia?" I asked. "I would love to go there."

"*Tja*," Mom said, looking at me askance. "Well, it might be okay to visit now, but when we were there in 1944, it was dangerous. Bandits, gangs, and partisans all around. Thugs, thieves. We didn't feel safe at all, but at least we were together. We especially didn't feel safe as young women. I was eighteen at the time. We were without my father. Your dad and his family were fatherless as well. All these families—women without men. These very young men were suddenly responsible for entire families."

"But you had your mothers," I said.

"*Ja*, we did. My mother was always a bit sickly and weak, so my older sister often took charge. On your dad's side, there was an uncle, Onkel Jasch, your Oma's brother, who took the lead. In fact, he led our entire village out of Russia and through Dresden and Yugoslavia. We would have been lost without him."

"Why wasn't he arrested in Russia?"

"He was, but he was one of two or three who came back, after about eight months. My father and your dad's father never returned after they were taken in February 1938. Oma Wall was just thirty-six years old, with six children, her youngest nine months old. She wore her hair in a long braid, which turned white practically overnight when he was arrested."

"That must have been so hard. To leave your village, not knowing what happened to your fathers," I said.

"We had no choice if we wanted any chance of survival. The Germans arrived in our village, in Nieder Chortiza, Ukraine, in June 1941, which made things better for us for a while. There was a bit more to eat; we were able to go to church again and celebrate Christmas and Easter. And to sing! We had almost forgotten what it was like to sing together. But then, in 1943, things got worse and worse. The Russians were advancing, the Germans planned their retreat, and we went with them. We all would have been killed had we stayed. The whole village packed up and headed west, away from the Russians."

"You must have been terrified."

She took a sip of raspberry juice and sighed. "*Ja*, I was scared a lot of the time. After 1938, there were hardly any men left in Nieder Chortiza. Most were very young, like your dad, in their early teens. We assumed our fathers had been banished to Siberia like my grandparents before them. We didn't know whether they were alive or dead. Escaping and surviving were the only things we could focus on, not on the missing. We had very little to eat. Potatoes, mostly, and bread, rarely. We had one cow, so we had a little milk as well. But there were four of us children, plus my mother."

"But wasn't the Ukraine known as the bread basket of Russia and maybe even of the world?"

"*Ja*, it was. The soil was rich and fertile. Most of the Mennonites had farms, and for a long time, we owned our own farms, but then the Russian government decided to collectivize everything and whatever we harvested belonged to the State. We worked the land, but couldn't keep any of the food. It was awful working the fields we had once owned and handing all of our harvest over. Everything went to the Russian officials. They must have laughed at us. Working our fingers to the bone and starving. Taking everything we had, for the greater good, they said."

"Were you able to have a little garden for your own family?"

"You know what we did? We grew potatoes. We kept scraps, you know, potato peel with just a little flesh so that we could plant them in the spring. My father dug a cellar underneath our cupboards so we could store more potatoes there. We only took out what we needed for the day, just in case officials knocked on the door, looking and scrounging for food. They actually came through our homes, went through our cupboards, and took everything they could find. It was horrible."

"You couldn't go at night and glean, you know, see if you could find any leftovers in the fields?"

She laughed. "Well, I suppose if you were brave enough. I would have been too scared. But before all of that, when times were good, we had a garden, enough to grow potatoes and tomatoes. Sometimes watermelons. Oh, they were so sweet." She laughed. "Just the best. So much sweeter than the ones we get here. In late summer or early fall, we would pickle watermelons and make watermelon syrup for the winter."

"I remember when watermelons used to arrive by the truckload in town here, at Funks," I said. "Remember? Those striped watermelons were so good. And huge! With *Rollkuchen* right out of the fryer—crisp and fresh and hot, with just a touch of icing sugar. My mouth is watering just thinking about that."

I looked around the kitchen, freshly baked white bread cooling on wooden racks, a big pot of *Borscht* on the stove, sour cherry jam cooling and lids still popping. Seven now.

"You know, when I was just eight years old, my father was kidnapped on his way home from work."

"What? Why?" I asked.

"At that time, in 1933, we had a bit of land, probably more than most. They called us '*kulaks*,' in this instance meaning wealthy peasants. My parents were also church deacons, but at that time, we weren't allowed to have church services or celebrate Christmas. We practiced our faith in secret. My mother hid her Bible under pillows or mattresses."

"So, all those promises made by Catherine the Great to the Mennonites years earlier when they emigrated to Ukraine from what is now Poland, to own land and have freedom of religion, didn't mean anything anymore."

"No, not a thing, not under Stalin."

"Wasn't there also talk of emigrating to Germany or Canada?" I asked.

"*Ja*, and maybe that is the real reason my father and others were arrested, because people thought they were collaborating with the Germans."

"I know you've told me these stories before, but every time I hear them, especially as I get older, they mean a little more."

Mom smiled, her fingers tracing the grooves in the cherry wood table. "Your Oma Sawatzky was a great storyteller."

"I remember. I loved listening to her soft, reflective voice. She never spoke about your father, though, my Opa. It even feels odd to say 'Opa' because I never knew him. But you must have been terrified when your father didn't come home that night," I said.

"I was scared. Father had the family ration cards with him, so when he was kidnapped, we had no food. It was a good thing he had dug a cellar underneath our potato cupboard. At least there was something to eat. When he was gone, my mother went to the prison in Zaporizhia to see if he was there, but was always told 'no,' until her brother-in-law suggested that the next time she went to the prison to drop something off for him, she should ask for a receipt. And imagine, the prison guard came back with a receipt and my father's signature. So at least we knew where he was."

"How long was he gone?"

"About eight weeks. It was just after Christmas that same year, in 1933, when he came home. I remember it so well. The four of us were huddled around the wood stove. It was bitterly cold. I heard something outside, footsteps. I was scared and pulled my little brother closer to me. The door opened and there he was. Wearing a great big coat, his moustache covered in ice crystals. My mother was in shock, tears rolling down her cheeks, laughing and crying all at the same time. We huddled around him.

"'*Hans, bist Du es wirklich?* Is it really you, John?' Mother said.

"He smiled a weary smile. 'I thought I'd never see you again,' he said.

"'What happened?' Mother said. 'Are you okay? You're so thin.'

"'Let's not talk about that now,' Father said. 'Let's just say a prayer of thanks to God.' He took off his coat, opened the door once again, shook off the snow and wet, and hung it near the stove to dry. Mother handed him a towel to dry his moustache. He looked tired and weary, but happy.

"'Come, children, let's hold hands.' We gathered around and bowed our heads. 'Heavenly Father, thank you for watching over my family while I was away and thank you for bringing me home so that we can all be together again. In Jesus' name, Amen.'

"'Are you here for good?' I asked him.

"'I hope so,' he said, touching my cheek. His hand was cold, rough, beautiful, and comforting.

"'We can have a little Christmas celebration, now that you're back,' Mother said quietly.

"'How about we sing a song?' he said. 'Katie, could you fetch my violin?'

"'*Ja,*' I said, and went into the other room to get it. 'Here you go.'

"Father breathed into his hands and rubbed them together before he took the violin. I loved it when Father played the violin. He closed his eyes and started to play '*O, du fröhliche,*' 'Oh, how joyfully.' We hummed and then sang along quietly. Music was in our souls. The Russians forbade religious practice of any kind, but music was in our bones. We looked at one another and smiled. I could feel the music resonating in my chest. From '*O du fröhliche,*' Father slipped into '*Stille Nacht.*' He played that last note and held it for a long time until it gradually faded away. We sat there, uttering quiet prayers of thanks. Interrupted by the rattling lid on the pot of boiling water, Mother got up to make tea. She had baked a few peppermint cookies for Christmas. She pulled those out of the cupboard and put them on a plate.

"I went to get the cups and cookies.

"'Papa, it's so good to have you home,' I said. He patted my arm and smiled.

"'How are you boys?' he said, ruffling their hair. John and Jake grinned from ear to ear.

"We slurped the hot tea and ate the peppermint cookies as slowly as possible. There were only a precious few.

"'It's late,' Mother said. 'Clear the table and let's go to bed. So much excitement,' she said, wiping her eyes as she turned away.

"The four of us—Irene twelve, I was eight, John six, and Jake four—all climbed into one big bed. The boys between Irene and me. Mother and Father were in the next room, speaking quietly.

"'What do you think they're saying?' I said.

"'Shhhhh,' Irene said. 'Be quiet, so we can hear.'

"I only heard '...*kulak*...church....hungry...no food...interrogation' and then the Lord's Prayer, '*Unser Vater, der Du bist in dem Himmel.*'"

Mom paused. She looked down, fingers tracing a pattern along the groove of the table.

"What was he like, your father? What do you remember about him?" I asked.

"He was a big man. Tall. Handsome. You know that little kink you have in your hair? I have it too, as does your brother," she said, running her fingers through her hair.

"That's from my father. He would have suffered a lot in prison. At least that first time he came back. Five years later, in 1938, he was taken again. It was February and so cold. Russian officials in black cars, dubbed 'the black raven,' drove through the Mennonite villages, knocking on doors, arresting our men. He never returned."

She stopped for a moment, staring out the window. "There were so few men left in our village of Nieder Chortiza. There were boys, like my brothers and your father. Your dad was only twelve, like me. This time, in 1938, his father was arrested, too. With the men gone from the village, everyone had to go to work in order to put food on the table. We stopped going to school. I really liked school, so that was hard. Your dad didn't like school; he was quite happy to be working the fields, with the horses."

"Did you ever hear from the men again?" I asked. "From your father?"

"We did. We learned that he had been taken to the prison in Zaporizhia, where he was previously held, just on the other side of the Dnieper River. My mother and other women from the village went to the prison quite often to deliver packages of laundry. They weren't allowed to bring food at that time. Then, later that year, in November I think it was, we were told he was no longer there, that he had been banished to Siberia to work in the labour camps, charged with collaborating with the Germans. We thought this might happen, but we were always so hopeful he would come back." She gazed out the kitchen window, taking in the view of Mt. Baker and its snow-capped peak.

She started to speak again. "You know, one time, I just felt so helpless, so powerless, I took some lime, spread it on our dirt floor, and with a branch, wrote the words '*Papa, komm bald nach Hause'*—Papa, come home soon—right into the floor. I told my brothers and sister that no one was allowed to walk in that space until he returned.

"My younger brother, John, stood at the side of the road keeping watch, hoping he would see Father coming home. There was nothing we could do."

The summer breeze blew in through the patio doors. A lid popped on the kitchen counter. I glanced at Mom, then down at the kitchen table, not wanting to break the spell.

"*Ja,* they took Father from me. I don't know where he is buried. I can't even visit his grave. You know, many years ago now, my mother, your Oma, told me that she saw Father in a dream. He was walking away from her, but then turned around to wave to her. At that moment, she knew he had died and that he was at peace. I think it allowed her to move on."

* * *

"Let's get back to Dad. Did you have your eye on him back in Ukraine, in your village of Nieder Chortiza?"

She laughed. "No, no. He was a bit younger than me, just by two months, but still, he was born in February 1926 and I was born in December 1925. We didn't really mingle with the younger kids."

"Even though you were only two months apart in age!"

"*Ja,* but we were in different grades in school. You know what it's like," she said. "You get teased when you play with younger kids."

"Yeah, I know," I said.

"We all used to go swimming in the Dnieper River. That was a lot of fun. Your Dad and I, we really only start-ed 'visiting' when we were all in Austria."

"Let's get back to that story," I said.

"*Ja*, so, as I said earlier, a few years after Father and many others were arrested and presumed sent to Siberia, the Germans arrived in our village. That was in June 1941. We heard German folksongs, heard our language being spoken—we were so happy. We felt protected. Germany and Russia were at war, but for a while there, things went well for us. We had more to eat and we weren't so scared all the time. But then, slowly, things started to change. The Russians were bombing villages and coming closer and closer to ours. They were pretty much across the Dnieper, so close we could see the flares from across the river.

"In October 1943, the Germans started planning their retreat. It was a beautiful fall, weather-wise. We had had a good harvest. The pear trees were laden with fruit, but there was dread in the air. The soldiers were getting ready to leave and we with them. We were terrified of being left behind. Our fun times on the Dnieper were long gone.

"We loaded our wagon with essentials, including po-tatoes from the cellar, a cooking pot, some flour, and our *Kroeger* clock. We had baked bread and buns leading up to the trek, so we had a little store of food to take with us. Night was falling. Up and down the dirt roads in the vil-lage, families were loading up their wagons, getting ready to leave. To flee. West, toward Poland, and then maybe to Germany. There was anticipation in the air, but we really had no idea what to expect. We had no idea where we would end up.

"I remember packing up what little clothing I had, even my Sunday dress, and a few things for my brothers. My mother and sister were packing up the food. I asked Mother where we were going and she just said, somewhat curtly,

'West. If we don't leave with the Germans now, we will be stuck here.'

"'How long will we be gone? Will we ever come back?'

"'Don't ask so many questions,' she said. She never yelled, but her voice was stern. 'The whole village is leaving.'

"My heart raced. 'What about Papa? We can't leave here. What if he comes back and we're not here?'

"Mother looked into my eyes and said quietly, 'Katie, I don't think he's coming back. None of the other men has returned. We haven't heard from your father in four years.'

"'Do you think he's still alive?' I asked.

"'We can only hope and pray that one day he'll return to us. If not, if he's gone, I know he's in the hands of our Lord and Saviour and we will be reunited in heaven. We must be brave. It's no longer safe for us to stay here. We have to stick together.'

"I could feel the tears welling up in my eyes. I turned away and kept packing. I couldn't bear the thought of my father, a big, strong man, diminished, tortured, possibly dead.

"As we began rolling out of the village, excitement and trepidation coursed through me. We didn't know what was in store for us. I turned to look back at our village. Out of the corner of my eye, I saw the tears rolling down Mother's cheeks. I reached for her hand."

* * *

"Was Dad's family with you as well?" I asked, jogging Mom's memory.

"Oh *ja*. Sorry, I was just back there in that moment. Yes, your dad, his mother, and his siblings were all on the trek with us. There was part of us that saw it as an adventure, exciting, but the bigger part was fear. And then, after a week or so, it was decided that the young men should carry on with the wagons and horses and the women and children should get on trains heading West. So, we were separated from our men again."

"All of these women alone with their children, not knowing if or when they would see these young men again. It must have been terrifying," I said.

"I don't think they had time to think about these things. The only goal was to escape the Soviet communists and end up somewhere safe and to see our loved ones again. We prayed every night for their safekeeping, wherever they were. After about three months of walking and travelling by train—more like crammed into cattle cars—we arrived in Dresden; the men and older boys a few weeks later. We never heard much about their journey over those two thousand kilometres. Maybe it was best we never knew. We were just happy they were safe. We were constantly on the move. From Dresden, we went to Yugoslavia and a good thing we did, because shortly after we left Dresden, it was firebombed. It wasn't long before your dad, amongst other young men, was drafted into the German army."

"But the Mennonites were conscientious objectors and peacekeepers," I said.

"That's true, but somewhere, somehow, before we were given permission to leave Dresden for Yugoslavia, it was agreed that when the young men turned eighteen, they would go into training for the German army."

"So, Dad, only just reunited with his family, had to leave again?"

"*Ja*, he turned eighteen in February 1944 and went to

army training camp in Yugoslavia. In the meantime, the rest of us, including your dad's family, moved to Austria. In October of that same year, he, along with many other young men, joined the German army. We stayed in Austria for three years. What a relief," Mom said, smiling. "I can't tell you how nice that was. To be somewhere where we felt safe."

"Did Dad know that all of you had left for Austria?" I asked.

"Yes, he had our Austrian address. From time to time, his mother would receive a letter. The two of us weren't writing yet," she said, smiling coyly.

"So, what happened on that day when you brought him home?"

"Oh yes, that was your original question, wasn't it? It was a Saturday and the tailor for whom I worked didn't need me that day. And it was market day, like I said earlier. I got up a little later than usual.

"'Morning, Ma,' I said as I walked into the little kitchen, which we shared with another family.

"'*Hast Du gut geschlafen*? Did you sleep well?' she said.

"'*Ja*, I did. You?'

"Ma nodded and continued stirring the porridge on the stove. 'Get me some more wood from outside, please,' she said.

"I stepped out onto the porch, grabbed some wood, and brought it in. Ma opened up the wood stove and tossed in a couple of pieces.

"'Are you baking today?'

"'*Ja*,' she said, smiling. 'I have flour today. Mrs. Koslowski brought us some milk this morning. And I still have a little yeast. Maybe we'll make buns. That will be a treat for the boys!'

"I smiled. It had been some time since Ma had had enough food and supplies to make her smile.

"'Once the work is done, can I go into town with Annie?' I asked.

"'Why?'

"'It's market day and it would be nice to do something different. Annie's Mom said she could go.'

"'I worry about you girls going into town on your own,' Ma said.

"'We'll be fine and we'll be home before dark,' I said. 'What are you worried about?'

"'Just watch out for the soldiers in town. The Americans are still here. You are pretty girls. Be careful. Don't want you to get into any trouble.'

"'We'll stick together,' I said. 'Maybe once the buns are done, I can take one or two with me? That way we'll have a little something to eat, in case we get hungry.'

"'Okay,' Ma said, 'but no more than two. Now, let's get the yeast going, otherwise the day will be gone before we get anything done.'

"I took a spoonful of yeast from the old tin, put it in a tall, white enamel coffee cup, added a teaspoon of sugar and warm water from the stovetop, and gave it a stir. In no time, it began to bubble and rise, filling the little room with that yeasty smell, with a promise of bread.

"'How much flour did you get yesterday, Ma?'

"'Enough to last us for a couple of weeks. I went to see Mr. Miller, the one who owns the flour mill. I traded in our clock for flour.'

"'Oh,' I said. 'I loved that clock. That is about all we had left from home. I always found it so comforting.'

"'I know, but it's okay,' Ma said. 'We have to eat. We

have to be practical. Get the milk, please. Let's heat it on the stove so that it's warm by the time the yeast is ready.'

"I went out to the cold room, grabbed the small, precious pail of milk, and brought it inside. Carefully, I poured one cup into a small tin pot. The stovetop was still warm. After a few minutes, it was scalding. Ma scooped out four cups of flour with her hands, put it in a large metal bowl, tossed in a teaspoon of salt, and ran her fingers through it. Then she added the yeast, which was about to spill over the cup, followed by the milk and a bit of melted butter.

"'We have butter?' I said. 'Where did you get it from?'

"'Mrs. Koslowski brought it yesterday, when she brought the milk.'

"'Wow! These will be good.'

"Ma had her hands deep into the dough now. 'One more scoop of flour and the dough will be perfect. Just sprinkle some on top here. There, that's it,' she said with a final pat. 'Let's cover this with a towel and let it rise.'

"I grabbed a clean dishtowel and covered the bowl.

"It was going to be a beautiful day. The sun was out, the sky was clear; there was a hint of fall in the air. It was the first time in many years that I wasn't afraid or on the run with my family and others from our village. We were always afraid we would be captured by the Russians and forced to go back. I thought about Father, blinked hard, and focused on the day.

"There was a knock at the door. I opened it. '*Tante* Wall,' I said, shaking her hand. '*Guten Morgen*! Good morning. How are you today? Isn't it a gorgeous day?'

"'You seem very happy this morning,' Tante Wall said.

"'*Ja*, Ma said I could go into town later today, once the baking is done. And you know what? I'm gonna bring your

Jacob home!' I said.

"'What are you talking about? Such nonsense. How are you going to do that? Have you heard from him?' Tante Wall asked.

"'No,' I said, 'but I just feel it.'

"'You young girls—fantasy—that's what that is,' she said, grinning, a twinkle in her bright blue eyes.

"'You'll see,' I said, laughing. 'Ma, Tante Wall is here.'

"Ma came out from the kitchen and shook her hand. They went out to the front porch to talk. Maybe there was news. They spoke in hushed tones.

"I went into the bedroom we all shared and looked for my dress. I wanted to get dressed up to go into town. There it was. My old Sunday dress. It was the only nice dress I had. A bit crumpled and wrinkled, but with a bit of pressing, it should be all right. I loved the floral pattern with its tiny, pale yellow and purple flowers. It reminded me of an alpine meadow. I held it up to myself. There was no mirror in the house, but I could see my reflection in the bedroom window and smiled.

"Jake sat up in bed. 'You look nice,' he said, rubbing his eyes. 'Where are you going?'

"'Annie and I are going into town,' I said.

"'Can I come?' he asked.

"'No. You and John should stay here with Ma.'

"'Hmmm. It would be fun to go to the market,' he said.

"'Ma's baking buns today!'

"'Really? Great!' He jumped out of bed.

"'They won't be ready for a while, but that's something to look forward to.'

"'I'll stay here and keep Ma company, don't worry,' he said. I bent down to tousle his hair. He was getting a bit big, but he was still my little brother.

"I picked up my dress and went back into the kitchen to find the iron. I grabbed it from the cupboard and placed it on the stovetop to heat. I pulled a towel from the same cupboard, put it on the rickety kitchen table, and placed the dress on top of it. I wet the tip of my finger with my tongue, picked up the iron, and tapped it. It sizzled. I blew on my finger. Slowly, I began pressing the dress. The alpine meadow came to life; the flowers danced before my eyes. Once the sash was pressed, I held the dress up, smiled, and placed it on a hanger.

"I set the iron to cool on the bricks. By this time, the dough had risen enough to punch it down for the second proofing.

"'Jake,' I called. 'Wanna punch down the dough?'

"'Oh yeah,' he said, coming into the kitchen. I removed the towel and he went at it, delighted to break the bubbles and breathe in the scent of yeast and flour and the promise of fresh buns.

"'How's it going in here?' Ma said as she came in the door.

"'Good,' I said. 'The dough is rising for the second time. Soon time to put the buns on the pans. I'll just get them ready for you.' I set about getting the baking pans out of the cupboard. We had found the pans in the house when we first arrived, left behind by other refugees. They were blackened with use. Nicely seasoned, well-used, and loved. I grabbed a bit of grease and prepped each pan. Ma wiped her hands and tested the dough.

"'Ready,' she said, and pulled off a section of the spongy dough. She held it in her left hand, expertly pinched off just the right amount, and placed it on the baking sheet.

And so on until the two sheets were full of perfect little dough balls. She put them in a slightly warm spot near the stove and covered them with clean towels. I couldn't wait. In about an hour, they would go into the oven, another half hour to bake, and then I could be off.

"I tossed another piece of wood into the stove. Ma opened the oven and felt the heat with her hand. 'I think it's hot enough,' she said, and placed the first pan into the oven. It wasn't long before the entire house smelled of baking. Just then, John came in from outside.

"'I was dreaming about bread,' he said. 'It smells so good in here. Are we really having fresh buns today?'

"'Yes,' I said, 'the first batch is almost done. We have fresh milk, too.'

"He grinned from ear to ear. It was all too good to be true. I could see it in his eyes; maybe he was thinking Papa would be home soon too. I didn't say anything.

"I opened the oven and turned the pan so that the buns would brown evenly on both sides. The smell was intoxicating. John was practically salivating.

"'Okay, one pan done. In goes the other,' I said, taking one pan out and shoving the other one in.

"It didn't take long and everything was done.

"'Ma,' I called. 'The buns are done. Can I go now?'

"Ma came into the kitchen. 'These look great! And so do you,' she said, looking at me in my freshly pressed dress. I didn't have pretty shoes, just an old pair of sandals someone was kind enough to give me. I had wiped and shined them up with a bit of grease and they looked all right.

"'Off you go,' Ma said. 'Take a couple of buns with you and remember what I said. Watch out for those American soldiers.'

"Annie was waiting outside and waved as I came out the door. She had taken care to curl her hair and put on a pretty dress as well. We linked arms and off we went, skipping.

"We were walking alongside the river, about halfway into town, when a couple of boys from our village rode up on their bicycles.

"'Hey, you two. Where are you off to?'

"'Town,' we said simultaneously.

"'Want a ride?'

"'What? On your bicycles?'

"'Yeah, just hop up on the bar,' Peter said.

"'Yeah, sure,' Annie said. I hung behind, just a bit. 'Oh, come on,' Annie said. 'Let's go. We'll get into town faster this way and save our shoes and feet.'

"'Okay,' I said, hopping onto Theo's bike, sitting sideways on the bar.

"We giggled and laughed uncontrollably as the boys zigzagged their way down the gravel road into town.

"'Here we are,' Theo said. I hopped off his bike and smoothed my dress. Annie was right behind me.

"'Can we treat you girls to a piece of apple strudel?' Peter said.

"Annie and I looked at one another and chorused 'Yes' at the same time. We didn't know how these boys could afford it, but didn't care. 'We'll share a piece between us,' I said, not wanting to appear greedy. The boys looked relieved.

"The apple strudel arrived, piled high with whipped cream. We couldn't stop smiling.

"'Thank you so much,' I said, laughing. 'It's so delicious.' It didn't take long for us to devour it.

"'And thanks again for the ride. We've got to get going now.'

"'Already? Where to? We can give you a ride back to the village.'

"'No thanks,' I said. 'We want to look around a bit. Thanks again.'

"Peter and Theo looked at each other, a bit puzzled and disappointed.

"'Let's go,' I said to Annie.

"'But I'd like to go with Peter,' Annie said.

"'We have to stick together,' I said. 'I promised Ma.'

"'You also told Tante Wall you'd bring Jacob home,' Annie said. 'What are the chances of that?'

"'Wait here a moment,' I said. 'I'm just going over to the water fountain to get a drink. I'll be right back.'

"I made my way through the crowd of people to the fountain. As I bent down to take a drink, I heard someone call my name. 'Katie, Katie!' I looked up for a moment, but couldn't figure out where the sound was coming from. Maybe I was just imagining things.

"'Katie! Trin!' I heard again.

"I looked up and there, coming down the hill, were two weary-looking young men, waving frantically, laughing and crying at the same time. Jacob and Daniel, home from the war.

"'How in the world?' I said.

"Jacob, tired and weary, with his telltale smile and bright blue eyes, picked me up and spun me around.

"'We were just coming over the hill when Daniel spotted your dress. He recognized the pattern and started pointing and shouting—'look, look over there'—and it was really you! I so hoped you hadn't all left Austria. Is my family still here?'

"'Yes,' I said, laughing. 'Your Ma came over to our house this morning and I told her I'd bring you home from town today. She laughed at me and told me not to talk such nonsense. And here you are! I can't believe my eyes!'

"'Is everybody okay?' Jacob said. 'All I could think about was seeing my family again and hoping everyone would still be here.'

"'Everyone is fine. Your mom, your sisters, your brother. All okay,' I said. Jacob let out a little yelp of delight and hugged me again.

"'But how...I'm so glad you found us,' I said.

"'Man, we were in a prisoner-of-war camp. For the last I don't know how many months, I was asked where I was from. I kept saying Austria, because that's the address I had. My German dialect didn't quite match up with the Austrian one, but after much to-do, I was released. I just prayed I wouldn't be sent back to Russia!'

"'Your family will be so relieved to see you. Here, I've got something for you,' I said and pulled a freshly baked bun out of my bag. 'And one for you, too,' I said to Daniel.

"'This smells like home,' Jacob said as he took the bun gently from my hands and inhaled deeply; home and warmth and love and family.

"'Let's go home,' he said.

"I went to find Annie, but she had gone off with Peter.

"Jacob, Daniel, and I slowly made our way back to the village. Once there, Daniel met with his family and I took Jacob to see his Ma.

"I knocked on the door, Jacob standing slightly off to one side.

"Tante Wall opened the door. 'Katie, back from town already?'

"I nodded. 'I have something for you.' Jacob stepped out in front of me. Tante Wall gasped, then laughed and cried and grabbed her son as if her life depended on it. *'Jacob, bist Du es wirklich?* Is it really you? *Kinder, kommt, schaut mal wer wieder da ist.* Kids, come look to see who's back!' Four sisters and a little brother came running. Laughing and crying as they embraced him.

"Tante Wall looked at me, tears rolling down her cheeks. 'You did it; you really did it,' she said. *'Danke, mein liebes Mädchen.* Thank you, my dear girl.'"

As Mom was telling me this, her eyes teared up.

"It's no wonder you and Dad started 'visiting' in Austria," I said. "Spotting you in the centre of town at the fountain like that. It must have stirred up all kinds of things in him!"

"*Ja,* many miles and many stories between now and then, too. For another time," Mom said. "I'm a bit tired now. Let's get dinner going."

"There's not much to do. We have bread and *Borscht* and fresh jam! A feast fit for a king," I said.

"What we would have given for a meal like this back then," Mom said, smiling, wiping her eyes.

Author's Note

It was October 1945 when Katie brought Jacob home, a year to the day since his conscription into the German army. Two years to the day, they fled Ukraine, and seven years earlier, the fathers of both Jacob and Katie were sentenced to be executed[1], not banished to Siberia as previously thought.

---

[1] *ВАЛЛ Яків Якович, 1899 р. народження, нар. і проживав у с. Нижня Хортиця Запорізького р-ну Запорізької області, німець, освіта початкова. Колгоспник к-спу ім. Калініна. "Трійкою" УНКВС по Дніпропетровській області 24 вересня 1938 року засуджений до розстрілу. Вирок виконано 7 жовтня 1938 року. Реабілітований у 1957 році. Місце поховання невідоме.*

[Yakov Yakovych WALL, born in 1899, was born and lived in the Village of Nyzhnia Khortytsia, District of Zaporizhia, Region of Zaporizhia, German, primary education. A collective farm worker of the collective farm named after Kalinin. On September 24, 1938, he was sentenced to be shot by the NKVD 'Troika' (special commissions of three persons of the Department of the People's Commissariat of Internal Affairs) in the Region of

Dnipropetrovsk. The sentence was executed on October 7, 1938. Rehabilitated in 1957. The place of burial is unknown.]

ЗАВАДСЬКИЙ Іван Якович, 1892 р. народження, нар. і проживав у с. Нижня Хортиця Запорізького р-ну Запорізької **області***, німець, освіта початкова. Рядовий колгоспник кспу “Інтернаціонал.” “Трійкою” УНКВС по Дніпропетровській області 10 жовтня 1938 року засуджений до розстрілу. Дата виконання вироку і місце поховання невідомі. Реабілітований у 1959 році.*

[Ivan Yakovlevich ZAVADSKY, born in 1892, was born and lived in the Village of Nyzhnia Khortytsia, District of Zaporizhia, Region of Zaporizhia, German, primary education. An ordinary collective farm worker of the International collective farm. On October 10, 1938, he was sentenced to be shot by the NKVD ‘Troika’ (special commissions of three persons of the Department of the People’s Commissariat of Internal Affairs) in the Region of Dnipropetrovsk. The date of execution of the sentence and the place of burial are unknown. Rehabilitated in 1959.]

Translation from the Ukrainian provided by ABC Translations.

Verbannte Mennoniten im Gebiet Saporoshje
16 Mennonitische Geschichte und Ahnenforschung
https://chortitza.org/Pis/Sapor.pdf, pages 5 and 16

SNOW DAY

"Let's go, everybody!" Dad shouted from outside. I looked up from the *Danny Orlis* adventure book I was reading to see Dad outside the kitchen window, dressed in his olive green work overalls and work boots, his heavy gloves held in one hand. "I'm gonna hitch up the toboggan and take you for a ride."

I quickly pulled on my black stretchy pants with the straps that fit under my feet so they wouldn't ride up. I hated the feeling of space between the tops of my socks and the bottoms of my pants, especially when everything got wet and the snowy bits crawled up in there and melted. I shivered at the thought. Heavy socks would help.

"Mom! Where's my ski jacket?" I shouted.

"Downstairs, where it should be, next to your winter boots."

"Okay," I said and ran down the twelve steps to the basement. Hanging next to the wood- and sawdust-burning stove were our winter jackets, and lined up in a shoe bin were all of our winter boots and barn shoes. It was the first big snow. Sometimes, we didn't get any snow, not a flake all winter long. It stayed wet throughout the winter, cold sometimes, but usually without snow. This morning, however, it was deep. I had heard them talking about it coming on CFVR, our local radio station. There was no sign of it last night, but there was a feeling of anticipation in the air. Maybe we wouldn't have to go to school. Maybe we could just stay home and drink cocoa and play or read.

That was just in storybooks. That never happened on the farm.

"C'mon BJ," I shouted to my little brother. "Let's go. Dad's waiting."

"Coming," he shouted back. "Just let me finish this bit I'm working on." He put the finishing touches on his Fisher-Price garage and came running down the stairs. He pulled on his puffy winter pants, heavy socks, boots, and jacket.

"Here's your toque," I said, throwing it at him. "And don't forget your gloves."

"They're so fat and clumsy," he said. "I can't feel anything when I've got them on."

"Here, take these," I said, tossing him a pair of knitted gloves with a nice warm lining.

"Where'd you find these?"

"They're mine. I got them for Christmas, but you can borrow them."

"But they're girl gloves," he said, "ew," and tossed them back to me.

"Tough luck, then. You're going to be freezing."

He looked at me shyly. "What are you gonna wear?"

"I've got another pair here. They're Mom's; I'll wear hers."

"Okay," he said.

I pulled my knitted toque on and laced up my boots. They were clumsy and awkward. I hardly ever wore them. The dirt caking them was likely last year's mud.

"Let's go," I said, and we trundled out the basement door. Dad had a big smile on his face.

"I've got the toboggan hitched up to the tractor," he said. "I'll take you for a spin around the field."

BJ and I looked at each other, big grins on our faces. We

walked down the snow-covered gravel driveway, through the open gate and into the field. There stood the John Deere, the CCM wooden toboggan hitched to it with a long piece of heavy rope.

"You go to the front," I said to my little brother. "I'm heavier, so I'll sit at the back and hang on to you."

"Okay," he said. I sat down behind him and hugged him. His body trembled with excitement.

"And, if I see that it's too hard for you to hold on to the rope, I'll reach over and grab on to it too. You'll be squished, though!" He nodded.

Dad climbed up onto the John Deere. "Ready?" he asked.

"Yup!" we shouted simultaneously.

He started the tractor, looked back at us, and said, "Okay, *los*," and slowly started driving. It took a few seconds for the toboggan to move. Once the rope grew taut, we began moving with it. I could hardly contain my excitement. I clung to my little brother, holding him and the rope tight and fast.

"Woo-hoo!" I shouted as we flew around the field in big circles. The cold wind stung my cheeks and eyes. Dad was whooping and hollering as we flew along. I could feel my little brother giggling with glee. I hugged him tighter. Dad picked up speed a little. Suddenly, I got a little nervous—I didn't want to go flying off the toboggan. I knew there was a little rise coming in the field, and just as the thought flitted across my brain, we hit it and the toboggan jumped a little, pulling me to one side. We kept going, flying through the air. I managed to right myself.

"Everybody happy?" Dad turned around to look at us.

"Woo-hoo, *ja ja*," BJ shouted. "Faster, faster!"

Dad accelerated a bit more.

"No, no, slow down," I shouted. I could feel myself sliding off again, and I didn't want to take my little brother with me. But if he stayed on, he might be too light and go flying too. Dad didn't hear me.

"Slow down," I shouted louder and louder. I could feel BJ tensing. Dad must have sensed something, even though he didn't appear to hear me. I could feel the John Deere gearing down. I relaxed, releasing my grip on my brother, and slid slightly to the left. Dad slowly drove back to the fence where we had started.

"Look at you two," he said, laughing as he hopped off the tractor. "Cheeks all rosy and fresh. Good, huh?"

"It was great, but a little scary when we went over that bump!" I said.

"I thought it would be a bit exciting. I would never let anything happen to you," he said, touching each of us on our cheeks. He unhitched the toboggan and handed it to us. "There you go. It might be fun to take it down that hill at the side of the house. I've got to get back to work now. Make sure the pipes haven't frozen and that the animals have everything they need."

"Thanks, Dad!" we shouted as he climbed back on the John Deere.

"Do you wanna do some more?" I asked BJ.

"Maybe a couple of runs. And then we could build a snowman."

"Good idea."

We trudged to the side of the house and up the hill. It was right beside my bedroom.

"Can I go by myself?" he asked. "I think maybe I'll go faster by myself. But you carry the toboggan up."

"Okay. Let's see how far you can go."

"Can you give me a push?"

"Sure," I said and pushed him as hard as I could. Down

the hill he flew, right into the garden.

"Woo-hoo!" he said when he got up. "See, I told you I'd go further without you."

"Let me try. You push me."

"But I can't push you as hard as you pushed me."

"Try!"

He slowly made his way up the hill, lugging the toboggan behind him. Once up, I climbed on and shouted "Okay!" He came from behind with a running start and pushed me. Off I went, but didn't get nearly as far as he had.

"My turn," he shouted from up top.

"Okay," I said, trudging up the hill with the toboggan.

"Now you come at me with a running push and see if I can go even further."

"Here I come," I said once he was situated and I was a few yards higher up. I ran as fast as I could with my heavy snow boots and threw all my weight into the push. He raced down the hill, bouncing along, until the toboggan came to a stop further into the garden, with him lying on his side, laughing so hard he could hardly contain himself.

"That was so great. Let's do it again!"

"No, let's not," I said. "I don't want you to get hurt. Let's build a snowman instead or make snow angels. Or both."

He got up and dusted himself off. "Here, take the toboggan," he said to me. I grabbed it, stood it up, stamped it on the snow-covered ground to get rid of the snow, and then pulled it up the hill. As I walked, something hit me from behind. There BJ stood, a big grin on his face, gathering up more snow and forming it into a snowball. The snow was just the right consistency to form the perfect artillery.

"Oh, is that what you want?" I asked, flinging the toboggan to one side and gathering up my own snow. Snowballs flew back and forth.

"How about a snow wash?" he said, laughing.

"No, thank you," I said, "please don't." But before I knew it, he was on my back, washing my face with a soft snowball.

"Ugghhh," I said, flinging him off my back. "I'm gonna get you!" I gathered up a handful of snow and started rubbing his face with it.

"Stop! Stop!" he yelled. "It hurts."

I stopped. "Poor baby," I said. "Can't take your own medicine?" It looked as though he was going to cry. "C'mon," I said. "Let's build the biggest snowman ever!"

"Okay," he said. We started rolling the snow, first as big as a snowball and then, as it gathered and rolled along, as big as a boulder.

"What do you think?" I said. "Is it big enough for the base?"

"Oh yeah," he said. "I'll start on the next one." In no time, we had the next ball. "Help me lift it onto the base."

Together we grabbed it and lifted. "And now for the face," I said. "How big?" He held out his arms to show the size. I began rolling it and we lifted it on top. "What shall we use for buttons and arms?"

"Do you think Mom would give us some buttons from her sewing kit?" he asked.

"Probably, but why don't we just gather up some rocks? Go down into the garden and dig a little bit. You'll find some there at the side."

He marched down to the garden and soon came back with rocks and some twigs to use for arms. "What about a hat?" he said. "Maybe we can use one of Dad's funny hats.

He doesn't like to wear hats anyway, so he won't mind."

"Yeah, sure, see what you can find."

He ran off into the basement and came back with a black cap. I placed it on the snowman's head. "Now we need a few pieces of rock or gravel for the eyes. Mom doesn't have any coal, does she, like it says in the song?"

"You mean, like 'Frosty the Snowman?'"

"Yeah, two eyes made out of coal."

"No, but we can find something else. And we need something for his nose."

"I'll go get something," he said. He ran off into the garden and started digging. A few minutes later, he came back with a carrot.

"You managed to find a carrot?" I asked.

"Yeah, I remember Mom saying they could stay in the ground a long time. Here you go."

"Why don't you do the honours?" I said. "Make a beautiful nose! And here, I've got some smaller rocks that might be nice for the eyes."

He placed the rocks and the carrot perfectly.

"Now what about his mouth? Let's get some pebbles and place them in a smile," I said. "And a scarf. Did you see an extra scarf in the basement?"

"Here, let's take mine," he said, removing his red and black scarf and wrapping it gently around the snowman's neck. "Look, Sis, isn't it great?"

"Beautiful," I said, patting him on the head.

Just then, Mom looked out the living room window and waved, laughing with glee at our snowman. She motioned us to her. Through the window, I could hear her say, "Cocoa!"

"Let's go," I said to BJ. "Mom's got cocoa waiting for us."

We ran into the basement, removing our wet clothing

and hanging it on the clothesline strung across the beams above the wooden stove. Mom had made a fire. The warmth filled the basement. I tossed off my heavy boots and placed them on old rags to absorb the wetness.

My hands and legs were red with cold. Chilled to the bone. We trundled up the basement steps and into the kitchen. On the stove, a pot of cocoa was almost bubbling. The skin was just about to form. I gave it a stir and stuck my nose into the pot. It smelled divine.

"Let me ladle that out for you," Mom said.

"It smells sooooo good, Mama," I said.

"Here you go," she said, pouring a huge ladleful into a mug. The pouring motion left a little froth at the top. I licked at it carefully. "And here you go," she said to my little brother, blowing on it gently. "Be careful. It's very hot."

BJ took his mug and went back to his Fisher-Price car garage. I took mine and settled back into my *Danny Orlis* book. Where would the adventures take me this time? Who would fall in love with whom?

SAFE HAVEN

The eggs felt smooth and comforting as I gathered and put them in the trays. Slowly, I pushed the wagon—which was custom-built just for me and my egg barn—up the long row. The stack of trays grew higher and higher until there were twelve. I pushed the stack to the back and started a new one. The rhythm was meditative and grounding, interrupted only by the occasional hen pecking at my hands.

Much as I grumbled and procrastinated getting into the barn after school, it was a place where no one bothered me. I turned up the volume on my transistor radio. "Here Comes the Sun" was playing. I loved that song and sang along at full blast. The hens fell silent. I looked around. Had something entered the barn? Then, the lone rooster crowed. A second later, the hens cackled so loudly, it was hard for me to hear the radio, never mind my own thoughts.

I went back to my rambling thoughts, now accompanied by "Tambourine Man." All my favourites were on today. There were strange things happening in school, in church, and in our small town.

"Are you going to the revival meeting tonight?" Marion had asked me.

"What revival meeting?"

"Have you seen that big tent set up in town? The Sutera Twins are holding evangelical meetings. You should come."

"Why?"

"To hear them speak. Renew your faith in Christ. Hear some good music. They play Christian rock."

I hated those kind of meetings. They made me feel like I was a horrible sinner; that I was bad.

Pastor Neufeld usually held revival meetings in our church over the course of an entire week. He was an enormous man, with curly, sandy blond hair and big glasses. Occasionally, he grabbed a handkerchief to wipe the sweat from his brow. Then he lifted his arm, shook his fist, and said in a booming voice: "Repent and sin no more. The second coming of Christ is near. Are you ready? ARE YOU READY?"

I was terrified. At the end of the sermon, he placed his hands on either side of the pulpit, slowly cast a glance across the congregation, and said, "AMEN."

As the organist softly played the hymn *"Just as I am, without one plea...oh lamb of God, I come to thee,"* another man of the church said, "If you feel God calling you, come forward. We will pray with you and you shall be saved."

One by one, a stream of people, young and old, trailed to the front of the church. There, they were met by prayer counselors and welcomed into the fold. I sat in the pew, hands clammy and sweaty. Wasn't I already saved? Didn't I do this last year? Why did I feel so guilty? Damn Pastor Neufeld. Oh no, I shouldn't have thought that. My heart pounded. Finally, the organist stopped playing that dreaded song and we bowed our heads in prayer.

I was used to those church revival meetings. There was a whole other breed of fanatics in town now. The Jesus People had arrived! Holy rollers and hippies all packed into one. Young bearded men wearing Jesus sandals and carrying cloth hippie bags. The women wore flowers in their hair, long patterned skirts, Jesus sandals, and patchouli. Everything was love and beauty. But not just that—"THE

END WAS NEAR!"

"I went to a gathering last night," Marion said to me in school that morning. "I prayed and prayed and suddenly, I was speaking in tongues. It was incredible. The Holy Spirit just washed over me and filled me with joy. It was like, wow, an incredible experience. And when it was over, I felt transformed."

"Oh," I said. I had been at home, doing my homework and practicing the piano.

"Someone had a vision that Christ is coming next week," she continued.

"But in the Bible it says we won't know the day He is coming," I said.

"Well, all I know is that the Holy Spirit was there last night, and it was VERY powerful. You could cut the air with a knife."

It was probably weed, I thought.

I was frightened. Everything was out of control. I looked around the barn and turned back to my task, picking up three eggs in each hand and putting them into the trays, getting lost in the rhythm again.

I longed to be amongst the city kids, seemingly unburdened with talk of "the end times" and all that. They lived their lives, went to parties, had boyfriends and girlfriends, danced, lived.

"Get me out of here!" I yelled.

The barn around me fell silent. The chickens didn't mind.

THE GREEN JACKET

I remember well the day my father died. It was Thursday, July 12, 2001. The Twin Towers were still standing. The Iraq war hadn't begun. Life as we knew it was plodding along, complacently so. But on that day, I was waiting for my best friend, Laura, to arrive from Winnipeg. That after-noon, we were going out to see Dad; the two of them got along famously. I picked her up from the airport and called the house to see how things were. No answer. I called my brother's cell phone. He picked up.

"Is he gone?" I asked.

"Yup."

"You should go," Laura said. "I'll stay here."

I picked up my daughter from daycare and headed out. There was nothing to do but be together. That evening at the house, nestled in the woods, the air was electrified. It was as though sparks flew amongst the trees; everything was abuzz. I felt his presence as we walked through the woods that summer evening—all of us: Mom, kids, grand-kids, in-laws. He had been in so much pain and now was free. It was like he was zipping through the trees, laughing his big laugh, his bright blue eyes twinkling.

At some point during the evening, Mom said, "You know, the other day, he went out into the woods by himself. I was a bit worried when I couldn't find him anywhere. His green jacket was gone, so I knew he was out. Then I saw him walking slowly along the driveway toward the house. He must have known it would be the last time he'd be out there. Saying goodbye to his beloved forest."

"He told me he wanted to die at home and be buried on this property," I said.

"He did? He never said that to me," one of my brothers piped up.

"But then he also told me that the city likely wouldn't allow it. He never mentioned it again."

Years later, as we were cleaning out the house, I came across the green jacket. There it was, the only jacket on the maple coatrack. It stood in the room we called the "bear pit," a cozy space in the lower level of the house, set apart from the rest of the room by two steps. A floor-to-ceiling stone fireplace covered most of the east wall. Remnants of the last bits of charred wood sat on the grate. I opened up the glass doors to the fireplace and inhaled the scent of wood smoke. A large wooden wheelbarrow stood next to the fireplace. A few pieces of kindling and three large birch logs lay at the bottom of the cart, along with a pair of well-worn men's gloves. In the centre of the bear pit stood a round custom-built table made from white maple, for playing cards or dominoes. At each of the four players' spots, there was a drawer with a small rack for dominoes.

The bear pit was the place where the men gathered primarily to socialize, play games, talk about old times, and sometimes discuss the latest news of farming, marketing boards, and, occasionally, politics. Separated from the bear pit by a wooden railing stood the pool table. I walked along it, running my hand over the worn green felt. I reached into one of the pockets and pulled out the cue ball. *Why not?* I thought. I picked up the rack, positioned it in the appropriate spot, and put the black ball in the centre, surrounded by striped and solid balls. I removed the rack, grabbed a cue stick, and chalked the tip with a hollowed-out blue chalk cube. I situated the cue ball just so, put the cue stick between my thumb and index finger, drew my right arm back, and aimed. With a resounding crack, the cue ball hit the rack of balls dead centre, sending the solid red into the corner pocket. Next, I went for the yellow striped ball, positioned perfectly for the centre pocket. It landed with a satisfying plop. One after the other, the balls landed in the pockets, sometimes using backhanded strategies to get the right angle, and sometimes shooting from one end of the table to the other. Satisfied, I put the cue stick back in its proper place and headed back to the bear pit.

I pulled the green jacket off the coat rack and breathed in its scent. I could still smell the English Leather Dad liked to use. I inhaled its warm, comforting fragrance. The collar was somewhat frayed, as were the knitted cuffs. The lining was red. I put my hands into the pockets, one at a time. In one pocket, I found a book of matches from Hy's Steakhouse. In the other, an open package of Halls cough drops, cherry flavoured. There were four drops left. I popped one in my mouth and held it against the roof of my mouth with my tongue. I sat down on the bear pit steps and held the jacket against my body.

Several weeks later, I met my brother for coffee. Surrounded by delectable bakery smells, freshly brewed coffee, and breakfast waffles, I said, "Do you still dream of Dad sometimes?"

"I haven't in a long time," he said, "but when I do, he's always wearing those green coveralls. You know, the ones he always wore when he was working outside or in the barn."

"Yeah, I know. I had a dream about him the other day. It was so vivid. I woke up crying. That hasn't happened in a long while. He was wearing that green quilted jacket, kind of like a ski jacket, but with a knitted collar and knitted cuffs."

"He always wore it when he went out for a smoke," he said, grinning, stirring his specialty coffee and licking the spoon.

"And when he went for his morning walks in the woods behind the house. I have pictures of the two of us in the forest with him wearing it. And a photo of him with Steph in the pick-up truck. She's sitting on his lap while he's driving. He used to do that to distract her while I was leaving the house," I said.

"He sure was good with the kids," he said. "I wish they'd had more time with him."

"Our relationship was never the same, you know, after I had her."

"What did you expect? You knew how he felt about his sister having a child out of wedlock during the war, how hard that was, and then he had to go through it all again with you."

"Yeah, but that was during the war. It's a bit different now, I would think."

"Not with his generation. Not with his peers. He was embarrassed. In his way of thinking, what you did reflected on him."

"You know what he said to me when I told him I was pregnant? He said I was degrading the family." Tears welled up in my eyes. I took a sip of my coffee, now lukewarm and disappointing.

"But you know," I said, "that's not what I wanted to talk about. When I woke up from my dream of him the other day, it was as though he was right there. Not like I hadn't seen him in almost seventeen years. He was right here, right now. And I was thinking about how much I loved and admired him and I wanted to share that with you."

He smiled. "I'm glad you feel that way about him, even though that time there was a bit rough."

"But that's family, right?" I said. "Through the good and the bad. In my dream, he said to me, 'I'll always take care of you,' and it was unbelievably comforting, as old as I am now. And he always did. He came when Steph was born, asked me if I had taken her home in a limousine. After all, his granddaughter deserved nothing less. I had to laugh, as I remembered the old Beck Taxi cab that took us home. He arrived at my house a few days later, walked up the stairs, and wrapped me in his arms. 'Did you miss my hugs?' he said. All I could do was hold him tighter."

"Family sure was important to him," he said.

"The church, too," I said. "He was always so involved with the church and with the MCC."

"Yeah, but I sometimes wondered if he was actually the big believer we thought he was."

"Really? What makes you say that?"

"It's just a hunch, but I think he was a bit disappointed in the church overall," he said.

"I think the rules of the church must have been a bit hard to take, once they arrived in Canada. No smoking, no drinking, no dancing. He loved all of that. Do you think the church was a bit surprised when I requested that the quartet play '*The Blue Danube Waltz*' at his funeral reception? I thought Dad would have loved that."

He grinned sheepishly.

"When JT spoke at Dad's graveside and said 'from Nieder Chortiza in Ukraine to the Fraser Valley,' I thought, wow—you just never know the journey your life is going to take. I mean, we've heard these stories of the Great Trek all our lives, but sometimes it just sinks in more than others."

"Look, I've gotta go," my brother said. "Do you want anything? Baguette, pastries?"

"No, I'm good. Thanks, though."

He settled the bill, chatted with the owner of the Patisserie for a moment, and offered me a ride home.

"Sure," I said. I climbed into his Range Rover. We didn't say much on the drive to my place. When we arrived, I said, "Can you wait a moment? I've got something for you."

I ran into the house, pulled the green quilted jacket out of my closet, and ran back out to the car. "Here," I said. "I know how close you were to him. You're his youngest son. You should have it."

He grinned and gave me a big, warm bear hug. Then he shrugged into the jacket, squirming slightly. "It's a little snug," he said, "but I'll take it."

HAPPY BIRTHDAY

"Tell me about the day I was born," my daughter said, looking at me sheepishly.

"And then you'll tell me you've heard it so many times before."

"Yeah, but it's a good one, so it's okay," she said, giggling. "Tell me as if it's the very first time and don't leave anything out."

"Well, there I was, the night before you were born, playing checkers with your Oma. She had come to help for a couple of weeks after you were born, but you were stubborn. She had already been at our house for almost two weeks, and you just weren't ready. Your due date came and went, came and went. In fact, that very morning, we had been to see my specialist, Dr. Amankwah."

"Who was as black as night," my daughter chimed in.

"Oh, he was lovely. It's true, I've never seen skin quite as dark as his and he was wonderful. So gentle and kind. Oma was with me. Dr. Amankwah examined me, speaking to you quietly as I lay there, saying, 'I know you don't want to come out. It's so warm in there, like Florida. But your grandma is here waiting for you and she's scheduled to go home tomorrow.' He turned to me and said, 'We'll schedule an induction for a week from now. If you deliver before then, great! Nice to meet you, Grandma,'" he said to Oma, and shook her hand.

"'Are you on call tonight?' I asked Dr. Amankwah.

"'Yes, I am,' he said.

"Oma and I walked down College Street to the subway, to catch the northbound train up to Yonge and Lawrence. You can imagine I really was nine months pregnant and waddling down the street. It was good to walk.

"After dinner that night, we settled into playing a game of checkers or many games, actually. Oma's a good player. I almost never win. That night, I could not be stopped. I won one game after another. Just before midnight, we called it quits. I was convinced you were going to incubate forever.

"I was just about to crawl into bed when the cramps started. Just twinges at first, like I was getting my period. I squirmed a bit, trying to get comfortable. Nah, it couldn't be time. Not yet. I wasn't ready! Another twinge, a little stronger this time. Water dribbling down my leg. How embarrassing. My water had broken. How many times had I heard someone say that, in the movies or in a story? It really does happen, just like that. I called my doula."

"Wait, you had a doula? You really are a hippie mom."

"Well, I wanted to have a midwife, but by the time I got around to looking for one, none was available. The next best thing was a doula."

"What do they do, exactly? And why?"

"You'll laugh. I had gone to these prenatal classes. You know Erika, my good friend from work. She came to these classes with me a couple of times. I assumed she knew that agreeing to attend these classes also implied, for me anyway, that she would accompany me through the birth. She looked at me with horror when I said that. Or maybe it was on the phone. I can't quite remember. In any event, during that last prenatal class, she suddenly felt quite unwell and told me that she would not be there for the birth."

"Wait. Where was Dad in all of this?"

"Not available," I said. "Not interested? I don't know. I'm sure he has his own story to tell, his own version. But he was so miserable during the pregnancy that I didn't want him around. Who needs all that negative energy? I needed all my energy for you," I said, pointing at her and smiling. "So, no Erika and I didn't know if Oma was coming, so I asked around for a doula. She would be there to take me to the hospital when the time came. She asked me if I had a birth plan."

"Seriously? A birth plan? You give birth. What's there to plan?"

"I know, it sounds completely hokey. I thought so too. But there she was, the doula, all dressed up, with her nails done just so, looking very professional. I can't quite remember her name. Judy, Linda? It was a common name. She had a clipboard and a form. I checked off 'natural birth,' 'no drugs,'— if at all possible, I added.

"'Would you like a mirror?' the doula asked.

"'Whatever for?' I said.

"'So you can see your baby being born.'

"'Oh, okay, that might be kinda cool,' I said."

"You actually saw me come out into the world?" my daughter interrupted.

"I did. Mind you, when the time came, I told them not to bother with the mirror. I must have been crazy when I opted for that, I thought.

"'You wanted it,' the doula said. 'Let's just bring it in.'

"And so there, in the birthing room, she brought in a mirror and held it up to the birth canal, shall we say, and there you were. Truly incredible."

"But wait, what was it like? Going through the birthing process? Did you really not have any drugs? It must have hurt like crazy."

"True, but it comes in waves. It doesn't hurt constantly."

"So go back. You were standing in your room and your water broke."

"Yeah."

"Did you call for Oma? What did she say?"

"I did call for Oma. Actually, I called the doula first."

"At midnight?"

"Yeah. Babies come at any time. They're not on a schedule. So, I called the doula and, of course, her first question, after I said 'My water broke' was, 'Are you sure?' I'm standing there with water dribbling down my leg. 'Yes, my water broke.'

"'How far apart are the contractions?'

"'I don't know. I haven't really timed them.'

"'Start timing them and call me back.'

"I walked into Oma's room to tell her my water broke. 'Are you sure?' she said.

"'YES!' I said. 'I've called the doula.'

"'Well, I better get dressed then,' she said.

"Just then, a much bigger twinge waved over me. I doubled over.

"'You okay?' Oma said.

"'Yeah, it just hurts. I'll call the doula again.' I dialled again. 'They're coming every ten minutes or so,' I told her.

"'Okay, I'm on my way.'

"'We'll be outside the house,' I said. I grabbed my overnight bag and headed down the stairs, Oma behind me. It was a nice spring night, just after midnight. A light rain was falling. The tulips were out in full bloom. I had seen them earlier in the day. We drove right past your dad's house on the way to the hospital."

"That must have been weird."

"It was," I said. "I was so torn about what to do. Call him and be greeted with 'oh yeah' or call him and be greeted with 'I'll be right there.' I had seen him two weeks earlier, or maybe it was longer. Time has a funny way of expanding and contracting in my mind. But I had seen him not long before this and I was kinda waiting for him to say 'Let me know when you go into labour,' or 'Let me know how I can help,' or 'Call me when the baby is born,' but he said nothing. Maybe he was waiting for me to ask? I just don't know. Like I said, he has his own version, I'm sure.

"As I was saying, we drove right past his house toward Women's College Hospital. When we arrived at the hospital, they put me in a wheelchair and brought me to a larger waiting area. Pre-birthing area, maybe. Oma rubbed my feet, my back. I think it was hard for her to see me in pain. But it passed. Wave after wave of it. Occasionally, a nurse would come by to see how dilated I was.

"In the early morning hours, they took me to a birthing room. Oma was right there with me. I was so grateful to have her there. And the doula. At one point, it just felt like too much. These cresting contractions were truly as they sound. Like a tsunami, ebbing and flowing, bigger with each wave. The doula assured me it would just be a few more. This was the very worst part. She was right. I was so hoping Dr. Amankwah would show up. And suddenly he was there, in the room. A big smile on his face, calling me a model patient. No drugs, everything natural. With a final push, there you were. A perfect little girl, very dark hair, like your dad, the bluest eyes, like mine and your Opa's, and your lips, a miniature replica of mine. It was a wonderful and strange sensation to see you, in the flesh, to meet you and to hold you, a part of me and yet very much your own person right from the get-go. You had the most beautiful ears, so delicate and intricate. Definitely not like mine, lucky you. You were so perfect and amazing. May 24, 1995, 8:13 a.m."

"And here we are, twenty-five years later," she said.

"And what a journey it's been!" I said, holding her close.

THE OLD CARDBOARD BOX

An unopened box with my name on it sat on my desk. Probably old college papers, concert programs, used airplane tickets, coasters, and matchbooks from European pubs I had visited. It smelled musty and old, having sat in Mom's basement for thirty-odd years, maybe even longer. Years ago, my father said to us, "You've still got boxes down here. Take them, please!" We all ignored his pleas.

I opened it and inside, along with the concert programs and airplane tickets, there were bundles of letters addressed to me. Letters from my Omas, my mother, even from my father and siblings.

I knew so little of my Omas' lives and there, in that box, was a little treasure trove of life, teeming with activity, hopes, and dreams—of lost dreams, too; of love and loss.

I took the top bundle and recognized my maternal grandmother's handwriting, her address in the top left-hand corner of the envelope. The stamp read 1973; that would have been my first year away from home, at college. "*Study hard,*" she wrote, "*education is something no one can take from you. I loved learning, I wanted to study, but I guess it wasn't meant to be.*" I sat back and an image of her flooded my mind's eye.

Oma sitting in her living room, glasses perched on her nose, reading. Anything she could get her hands on. Sometimes in German, sometimes in Russian. If she wasn't reading, she was crocheting doilies, any pattern she could find, always eager to learn something new. Her face crinkled like a furrowed field when she smiled. She was only seventy-nine at the time, but I think she had lived several lives by then. Born in Ukraine, journeying across Europe, finally reaching the west coast of Canada in 1955.

Having hoards of grandchildren over for perogies and farmer sausage gave her immense pleasure. She divided the groups of grandchildren into ages. One week she invited high school kids, the next elementary school-aged kids. We squeezed around her kitchen table, covered in a yellow floral oilcloth tablecloth. The gas stove sat opposite the table. Her house always smelled slightly of gas and I worried that one day the house would burn down with her in it. Miraculously, it didn't. We sat around that table and chatted amongst ourselves about the goings-on at school, in English. I don't know how much English Oma actually understood. Probably more than we thought. She sat quietly and took it all in, watching with joy as the platters of perogies and sausages disappeared as quickly as she put them on the table. There were always peppermint cookies around Christmastime and iced and decorated Easter bread called *Paska* in the spring.

Oma's house on Birch Street was the place to be for the Easter egg hunt. With twenty-three grandchildren, the colourful eggs were hidden, found, and hidden again so everyone had a chance to do the hunt. She didn't mess with chocolate. Farm fresh eggs were hard-boiled and dyed for the occasion and, once found, turned into egg and potato salad. The tall grasses and the weeping willow tree in her backyard made for terrific hiding places. Oma loved Easter.

I continued looking through the letters and found several Easter cards. In one of the cards she had written, *"When you're old, you'll remember the Easter stories I told you as a child."* My eyes welled up with tears. Peter and the Easter

Bunny came to mind. He always wanted to find the Easter Bunny and watch him colouring the eggs and hiding them. She was soft-spoken and held our attention with her voice. And when she'd come to the end of the story, she would laugh until the tears rolled down her wrinkled cheeks. Perhaps laughing at her childhood self. I looked at the Easter letter again and read, *"and here's one dollar from the Easter Bunny."*

Oma's house was headquarters for Hallowe'en too, because she lived in town. She didn't care for "trick or treat" because it reminded her of the poverty she had suffered in Ukraine and it seemed like begging. "You don't have to beg in Canada," she'd say, and this sentiment was echoed by our parents. But she loved to have us around, so it didn't matter. We dumped our things at her house. Donned old sheets with cut-outs for eyes and nose and became ghosts— or dressed as farmers—and off we went around the few blocks near her house to fill our flour sacks with treats. Back at her house, we sat and sorted and traded our treats. She always had traditional Hallowe'en molasses candies in her pantry for us and welcomed the kids in the neighbourhood.

I grabbed another letter. A one-dollar bill floated to the floor. I laughed aloud. I read the letter, this one dated October 1973, in which she wrote, *"and I'm sending you a dollar for 'Holoven.'"* It took me a second to read the word phonetically and then realized it was "Hallowe'en."

As I continued reading through the letters, now dated early November, there was talk of Christmas, buying presents, and preparations for the big gathering. Oma loved Santa and told stories of how utterly shattered she was when she realized that he wasn't real.

She never spoke about her husband, my Opa, arrested by the Russians in 1938 for the second time, never to return. We knew the story of how he had returned just after Christmas, after the first time he was arrested, his moustache covered in winter frost. And every Christmas, to be reminded of his absence. Oma's house was the last stop on our caroling route. As we gathered on her front lawn and started singing, she came to the window, parted the curtains, and looked out, her black-rimmed glasses perched on her nose. "*Stille Nacht*" ended the evening.

As demure and quiet as my maternal grandmother was, my paternal grandmother was loud, boisterous, and quick to criticize. Both lost their husbands to the Russians in the same raids. Both traversed Europe and ended up in Canada. They all talked about the Great Trek from Russia *ad nauseam* and as kids, we had had enough. As I read the letters, though, I marvelled at their strength.

There were only a handful of letters from Oma Wall. She died during my first year of college. I was almost finished that year and in the last two letters, written at the end of March and early April 1974, she asked if I was coming home soon, for Easter. Two weeks later, she died.

A couple of months later, I left for Europe for the first time, travelling with my mother. In Salzburg, I heard "*Ein deutsches Requiem*" by Brahms for the first time, conducted by Herbert von Karajan. There we were, the two of us, my mother and I, both dressed in brightly coloured long summer dresses, while the rest of the audience was dressed in black, listening to the words:

"*Selig sind, die da Leid tragen, denn sie sollen getröstet werden...Tod, wo ist dein Stachel?*"

"Blessed are they that mourn, for they shall be comforted... oh death, where is thy sting?"

The music penetrated my entire being right from the first note. I cannot listen to this requiem without thinking of my Oma Wall. She had a big laugh, a big heart, and big faith. She left a big void.

Two women, pillars of my life, as different as night and day, with hearts full of love for us all. Between them, they told us so many stories. And I know that if I know this much, there must be many more stories untold.

---

* A version of this story was originally published in Roots and Branches, Periodical of the Mennonite Historical Society of BC, in the September 2022 issue, Volume 28, No. 3, pp.12-14.

ST. PETER AM KAMMERSBERG

The little red Opel hugged the narrow mountain road. Late spring snowflakes fell lazily from the sky.

"So, this is the mountain your mother didn't want you to hike with that boy?" I asked Mom. She laughed nervously, holding on to the door grip as a tourist bus squeezed past us. "*Ja! Der Großglockner!*"

"Who was he?"

"Just a boy from the village."

"From the old village in Russia or St. Peter in Austria?"

"St. Peter."

"Does he still live here?" We had arrived in St. Peter the day before.

"I don't know. I don't even remember his name," she said.

It was snowing harder now, huge flakes swirling around us. "We should turn back," Mom said to Alf. "The roads are too dangerous."

At the next pullout, on the side of the precipice, he managed to turn the car around. Partway down, the road was clear and alpine flowers in bursts of blues, pinks, purples, and yellows appeared around every corner. Before long, the village came into view. A cluster of homes, a pub, and our *Pension* nestled in a little enclave, surrounded by mountainside farms. We were going to stay here for a few days.

"Your dad used to work for one of those farmers up the mountain," Mom said. "His name was Farmer Moa."

"We could ask, in the local pub, if he's still around," Alf said.

"*Ja*," she said.

We dropped the car at the Pension and walked across to the pub. It was midday and some of the locals, mostly men, were seated on barstools, having a beer.

"*Grüss Gott*!" the bartender said as we walked in. "What can I get you? Beer?"

"Sure," Alf said.

"And for the ladies?"

"Apple cider," I said. "Two, please."

"Only the best in town," he said, sliding a beer toward my brother and pouring two tall glasses of cider.

I took a sip of the cold drink. Ice cold, carbonated, and slightly alcoholic. I turned to Mom. She took a big sip and looked at me with surprise. "I think there's something in this," she said.

"Where are you folks from?" the bartender asked.

"Canada," Alf said.

"Canada! *Mein lieber Gott. So weit weg*," he said, shaking his head.

"My mom and dad lived here after the war. Do you know a farmer by the name of Moa? My father worked for him."

"*Ja, freilich.* He died a while back," he said, crossing himself. "His wife and sons still live up the mountain."

"We wanted to go see them. Do you think that would be all right?" my brother asked.

"*Ja, ja,* just follow that path up the mountain and knock on the door. They would be thrilled to see you. Canada," he said, shaking his head. "Such a long way."

"Ready to do some hiking?" Alf said, looking at me and Mom.

"*Freilich.* Let's go," we said.

We walked down the road, turned left as instructed, and headed up the mountain. I grabbed a stick along the way and handed it to Mom. We huffed and puffed toward the small house at the top of the mountain. The grass was high all around us. As we got closer, Mom took the lead, walked up to the solid wooden door, and knocked. A dog barked. I heard footsteps shuffling toward the door. I looked at my brother and grinned with nervous anticipation.

The door opened. A short, plump woman with dark, greying hair pulled back in a bun stood there, looking at us quizzically. "*Grüss Gott,*" she said. She wore a faded black dress, belted at the waist, and felt slippers.

"*Grüss Gott,*" Mom said, extending her hand. "My husband, Jacob, worked here right after the war."

"Ah," she said, "there were many who came."

Mom pulled out a photo of our dad.

"*Ach, mein Gott,*" she said, clasping her hand over her mouth. "This is your husband? Come in, come in."

She opened the door wide. She motioned for us to sit at the heavy wooden table. The floor was made of packed dirt.

"Peter!" she shouted. "Hans! We have company. From Canada."

Within moments, two strapping young men in their late twenties or early thirties appeared.

"Fetch some *Apfelmost,*" she said, "and *Speck.* I will cut some bread. Canada," she said again, clapping her hands. She turned to Mom. "These are your children?"

"Yes," Mom said, introducing us. "Betty and Alf."

She clasped each of our hands in turn. Her hands were

worn and wrinkled, the nails short and lined with dirt. She grinned, a couple of teeth missing.

"Oh, Jasch, he was soooo handsome. All the girls liked him," she said.

I looked at Alf and grinned, stifling a giggle.

The boys returned with a jug of apple cider, a big wooden cutting board laden with Speck, which was ninety percent lard, and the tiniest strip of ham. Thick slabs of dark, heavy bread sat beside it.

"*Tja, mein Mann*, God rest his soul," Mrs. Moa said, crossing herself, "died a few years ago. Right in the field. Peter found him." Peter and Hans, both sitting at the table, looked down. "Good thing I've got these big boys to help with the farm. Peter needs a wife," she said, looking at me.

I pretended not to understand. I looked at Alf. He chuckled. "Listen to her," he whispered to me in English.

"You should stay here," Peter said.

"I need to go home to Jacob," Mom said. "He's waiting for me."

"Not you," he said, "the young one."

There I was, eighteen years of age, my thick auburn hair in braids, tall and robust. A farmer's wife indeed. I felt myself blush.

"Eat, eat," Mrs. Moa said, and handed each of us a one-inch thick piece of Speck on an equally thick slice of bread.

"*Danke*," I said.

"*Ach*, you speak German?" she said, laughing. "That's perfect."

"*Ein bißchen*," I said.

Hans poured a glass of *Apfelmost* for each of us. I sank my teeth into the Speck and almost gagged. The flavor was smoky and nice, but the texture...! I chewed and chewed, then took a big gulp of cider. My head buzzed. Alf looked over at me and saw me struggling. Under the table, he showed me his napkin. He had already placed his partially chewed Speck into it and motioned for me to do the same. I tried to do it discreetly, when it fell out of my hand. Within seconds, the dog scooped it up. Mom, meanwhile, ate her whole piece and downed the glass of cider.

"What's Jacob doing in Canada?" Mrs. Moa asked.

"Farming," Mom said.

"Like here?" she said. "In the fields?"

"Well, yes, but mostly chickens. We have thousands of laying hens."

"Thousands? How is that even possible?"

"It works," Mom said, without going into detail.

"And with chickens and eggs, you can make enough money to fly here from Canada?" She shook her head in disbelief.

Mom looked at the two of us. I could sense her discomfort. "Well, shall we get going?" she said a bit abruptly.

We nodded and made to get up.

"You're going already?" Mrs. Moa said. "Let me give you some bread and Speck to take with you."

"That's all right," Mom said, "thank you."

"You're not staying then?" Peter said, looking at me.

"She has to study," Mom said.

"Say 'hello' to Jacob," Mrs. Moa said, taking Mom's hands in both of hers.

Halfway down the mountain, Alf opened up the napkin he had stuck in his pocket and flung the remaining Speck into the fields.

"I couldn't do it," he said.

"We were very grateful for Speck and bread after the

war," Mom said sternly as she marched down the hillside ahead of us. "Once you've starved, you're very thankful for a bit of grease and bacon."

"Hey, Mom," I said. "Thanks for not leaving me behind with Mrs. Moa and her sons. Can you imagine?"

Mom laughed. "It would be a very hard life. *Mein lieber Mann!* You would be running for *Mama* and her boys. No chance for an education or an easier life."

"You must be happy you're in Canada. With chickens and all."

"*Das kann man wohl sagen.* You can say that again. But the Austrians were good to us. Very good."

---

*A version of this story was originally published in Roots and Branches, Periodical of the Mennonite Historical Society of BC, in the September 2019 issue, Volume 25 Number 3, pp 17-18.

THE KROEGER CLOCK

In 1945, two years after fleeing Ukraine, my mother, her two brothers—John and Jacob—her sister Irene, and my Oma arrived in St. Petersburg with their few possessions, the Kroeger Clock amongst them. It had travelled with them through Poland, Dresden, and Yugoslavia, finally arriving here, in this little Austrian village, never missing a beat.

Thirty-one years later, in 1974, my mother, brother, and I were in St. Peter am Kammersberg when the story of the clock resurfaced.

"Mom, didn't you tell us that Oma Sawatzky exchanged a family clock for flour so she could feed you guys?" Alf said. "Maybe we should try to track it down."

"Oh, *ja*," Mom said, "that was around here too."

"Do you remember with whom she made the trade?"

"Yes, the owner of a flour mill. Somewhere along the river," she said.

"Shall we go to the local information source?" Alf said.

"You mean the pub?" I said.

"Yup!"

"I'll stay here," Mom said. "I'll wait in the car. You go."

In mere moments, Alf came out of the pub and said, "Let's go!"

We climbed back into the Opel and off we went.

"So, where are we going?"

"The guy in the pub says the owner of the flour mill now lives in the next village. His name? You guessed it. Mr. Miller!"

We drove down the dirt road, along the river, in the direction the pub owner had indicated. Train tracks ran next to the river. A little train, just three cars, was travelling beside us, its bell clanging.

"Nothing has changed here in thirty years," Mom said. "Nothing. We used to travel from village to village on that little train. We called it the *'Bimmelbahn.'*"

"I couldn't live here," I said. "No school, no library. Where do these kids go to school?"

"I think the Catholic Church runs a school," Mom said.

"Here we are," Alf said.

"What do you mean, 'here we are'?" I asked.

"In the next village."

It was hard to tell where one village ended and the next began. In each village, there were a few farms, and one or two buildings housing a little grocery and a post office.

"You must have missed the last sign that read *'Ortsende.'* Town's end."

"I guess," I said. "Into the pub?"

"Yup."

Within minutes, he was coming back to the car and pointing down the road to a little house. "That's where Mr. Miller lives," he said. "We can just walk."

We climbed out of the car and walked along the river. A water wheel stood beside the stone house. An elderly gentleman tinkered with it. He looked up as we approached.

"Grüß Gott," Mom said.

"I remember that clock," Mr. Miller said once Mom had told him the story of their trek through Europe and arrival in Austria. "It ran exceptionally well. I felt badly taking it from your mother," he said, looking away and shaking his head. "How is she? Is she still alive?"

"Oh *ja*," Mom said. "She lives in Canada now, near us."

"Canada?" he said, shaking his head. "So far away."

"Can we see the clock?" my brother asked.

"I wish I could show it to you, but I no longer have it," Mr. Miller said. "I sold it to a doctor a few years ago, a clock collector."

"And where does he live?" we asked simultaneously. "In the next village?"

"Yes!" He gave us directions and off we went. It was turning into a bit of a treasure hunt.

We arrived in the next village, parked the car on a steep angle, and walked up the front steps. The house was one of many row houses, each adorned with flower boxes filled with bright red- and salmon-coloured trailing geraniums, interspersed with daisies.

Alf knocked on the door and a woman in her mid-fifties opened it. She wore a smock over her dress, a tea towel in her hand.

"*Ja?*" she said.

"*Grüß Gott*," Mom said, stepping in front of Alf. She explained our search for the clock and asked if her husband still had it.

"I don't know about that specific one," she said. "He has many clocks."

"May we take a look?" Alf asked.

She opened the door somewhat reluctantly and let us step inside.

There on the wall hung about fifteen clocks.

"There it is!" Mom said, pointing to a flat-faced wall clock with a pale green background and an intricate painting of a pastoral scene. Long chimes. It looked perfect.

"*O ja*, that one," she said, smiling. "My husband says

of all the clocks, that one, that one never stops working or needs repairs. It just keeps going."

"Do you think your husband would sell it back to us?" my brother asked.

She shrugged her shoulders. "You'd have to ask him. He's still in the clinic."

Just then the back door opened. In walked a short, dark-haired man wearing a beige suit, a pocket watch in his vest pocket, black-rimmed glasses, and a fedora.

"Ah, you're home," the woman said.

"*Grüß Gott,*" he said, shaking each of our hands in turn.

His wife explained our story to him. He listened and nodded attentively.

"So, what do you say? Will you sell it to us?" my brother asked again. "This clock is a family heirloom, traded so my Oma could feed her family."

He cleared his throat. "It's worth a lot of money," he said.

"It would mean a lot to us," Alf said. "It was one of the few possessions my Oma was able to take with her on that long trek across Ukraine to Poland, Germany, Yugoslavia, and finally to Austria. It has survived all of that. It would be wonderful if we could take it home to her. We're happy to pay."

"No," he said, shaking his head. "I can't part with it."

"Are you sure?" Alf said.

Mom didn't say anything. She just looked at the clock.

"This wasn't our original clock," she said.

"What?" we both said.

"I mean, it is the clock I grew up with, but I remember that, when I was about five, everything we owned, including our Kroeger clock, was sold at auction. We were completely dispossessed. It was punishment of sorts, under the guise of increased taxes levied by the authorities, likely because my father was a deacon and involved in the church. That night, after the auction, some of our neighbours, who had bought a few of our things, snuck them back to us, but the clock wasn't amongst these items. And, you have to understand, a Kroeger clock, handcrafted by local tradesmen, made a home complete. Sometimes given as wedding gifts. Oma was very grateful when sometime after the auction another family gave us this clock, which became a fixture in our home when I was growing up."

The doctor listened intently as Mom told us this story in German.

"You see," Alf said, looking at the doctor. "The clock has a lot more stories to tell. You sure you don't want to part with it?"

The doctor smiled, lips pursed, his right hand in the pocket of his vest, but didn't say anything. Perhaps thinking, *It's becoming more valuable all the time.*

"*Na ja*, well," Mom finally said, looking at my brother and me. "Shall we go?"

We thanked the doctor and his wife for the visit and left, feeling rather deflated after the big chase. The hunt had been a success, but who wants to leave without the treasure?

As we headed back to the *Pension* in St. Peter, Mom told us a little more about the clock and its story.

"I didn't know the clockmaker trade was a thing amongst the Mennonites," I said.

"*O ja*," Mom said. "It goes way back to when our forefathers lived in Poland, in Gdansk, and was passed on from generation to generation. Some of the clocks had elaborate decorations with detailed paintings of biblical scenes. As you saw, ours had a pastoral scene. It always gave me a sense of comfort, especially when my father was gone." She paused. "*Tja*, well."

In 1987, thirteen years later, my mother's brother sought out the clock and offered to buy it. Again, the doctor refused to part with it, only this time, he followed up with a letter, saying he was prepared to sell it for six thousand Canadian dollars. My uncle declined. And that's where the journey ends...for the time being.

THE
PASSPORT

"Do you know where my passport is?" Mom asks, her voice small and weak on the other end of the phone.

"I do," I say. "It's in the hall closet, in a box. Next time I come over, I'll double-check to make sure that it's there."

"I don't think it is," she says.

"Do you need it?" I ask.

"Well, I don't know if I need it, but someone asked me if I wanted to go to Paraguay on a tour, but I don't know if I should."

"Oh," I say. "When?"

"Well, that's the thing. I don't know exactly."

"Don't worry, Mom, we'll sort it out for you."

"Okay then, bye."

I hang up the phone. I feel sad and oddly maternal toward my mom. There's something that feels so wrong about that, but, at the same time, how else could it be?

On Saturday, I hop in the car and head to Mom's, not knowing quite what to expect. Springtime on the farm is always glorious. As I pull up the cedar tree-lined driveway, I see the rhododendrons starting to appear. The first bushes are red, the next a dark pink, and, in the distance, the whites are showing through. Everywhere I look, things are waking up.

Mom is sitting outside with her care aide, Wendy. My heart stops just a little.

"Hi Mom," I call out. My voice sounds a little too exuberant, but I can't help it. She waves and smiles. "How are you? Do you want to go for a little walk?"

"Yeah, we can," she says.

"I can manage," I say to the caregiver.

"You sure?"

"Yup, it's no problem. We'll take the walker and we'll be fine," I say.

We make our way down toward the mailbox. "What's new?" I ask.

"There's this tour to South America and I'm not sure whether I should go or not."

"You've been to South America. Do you want to go again?"

"Not really," she says. "It's awfully hot down there. You know, when our people left Europe for Paraguay, they had a very hard time. The extreme heat, no refrigerators, chopping down the jungle so they could grow crops. I'm so glad we could come to Canada."

"Me too," I say. "I don't think I would have liked growing up in Paraguay! You didn't have an easy time of it either, clearing land to make room to grow berries and build barns."

"*Ja*, that's true."

We walk in silence for a bit.

"Remember that first trip we took together to Europe? We went to that little Austrian village of St. Peter am Kammersberg. You wanted to see the old tailor you worked for."

"Yeah, it hadn't changed a bit. That bright yellow house we lived in was exactly as we left it. But the old tailor had died. We saw his son Freddy. He had this cleft lip, I remember," she says. "He was so shocked to see me and to see you and your brother! He just couldn't believe it."

"That was pretty neat," I say. "And then, the visit up

to the old farm where Dad used to work? Remember how Mrs. Farmer Moa couldn't stop talking about how handsome dad was and how all the girls liked him?"

"And her son wanted you to stay there in St. Peter and marry him," she says and starts laughing. "Can you imagine? You living on that farm, in that house with the dirt floor, serving that man?"

"I'm so glad you told him I had to go back to school," I say, laughing.

"He didn't think girls should be going to school. What for?" she says, bursting into fits of giggles again. "Don't need no education to sweep a dirt floor and cook for the men."

"Yeah, and the food. She was so eager to ply us with homebrewed apple cider, heavy rye bread, and *Speck*—a big cut of bacon that was mostly lard," I said.

"Food fit for a hard-working man," she says. "Oh, that son of hers loved your youth and your braids. Wanted you to stay," she says again, laughing.

"I couldn't get down that hill fast enough," I say. "It was beautiful up there, though. So lush and green. I can see how Dad would have enjoyed being there."

"Oh, the Austrians were so good to us. Gave us shelter, work, and food," she says, nodding.

"We've been on some pretty great trips together, you and I," I say, putting my arm around her. "Remember when we went to Italy?"

"Oh yeah, that was a last-minute trip. Weren't you supposed to meet your dream man there? There was something like that. I remember you were heading off to Salzburg for the music festival and then to northern Italy. There was a house we could stay in," she says.

"Yeah, Fred, he was supposed to meet me in Italy. I

thought he was the one for me, only to find out he was living with another woman."

"It worked out well for me!" Mom says. "Didn't we drive from Vienna to Italy?"

"Yes," I say, "and you wrote down how many tunnels we travelled through. I think there were at least twenty-five."

"There was a lot," she says.

"That house in Bibione was a bit creepy, though, wasn't it? Actually, it was probably quite nice, but we were afraid to really live there for that week. I'm not sure why. We were nervous, I guess."

"There were those funny sounds at night," she says. "It sounded like someone was tossing a ball around upstairs in the attic."

"I know," I say, laughing. "I remember. I was picturing squirrels tossing nuts back and forth. We never figured it out."

"But I got so scared in Italy," she says suddenly.

"Why?"

"That day when we were at the beach, at the Adriatic Sea. I went for a long walk."

"You know what I remember? All the women were topless at the beach and you and I didn't have our bathing suits. You whipped off your shirt and went for a walk wearing your Playtex bra and a pair of shorts," I say, laughing.

"Oh yeah," she says. "But then, I walked and walked and walked and I couldn't remember where you were. I couldn't find you."

"I remember thinking you were gone for a long time, but I was absorbed in my book."

"I was never as happy as when I spotted you in that

lounge chair, happily reading away."

We were heading back up the driveway now. "Look at the wisteria," I say. "It's almost in full bloom. Just glorious."

"What's the name of it again?" she asks.

"Wisteria," I say.

"That's a hard word to say."

"Not as hard as rhododendron!"

We round the corner on the driveway and head toward the garage entrance of the house. Wendy is waiting for us.

"Oh, there you are," Mom says.

"Did you have a nice time?"

"Yes," she says, looking at the flowers and enjoying the sunshine. "Let's go in and have some tea."

They make their way slowly up the last few steps into the house. I put the kettle on and wait for them to come back from the bathroom.

"I didn't bake anything," Mom says as she walks into the kitchen.

"No problem, I brought cherry pie," I say.

"Oh, that looks good," she says, her eyes wide and smiling. "I'm going to enjoy that."

It wasn't long ago that there would have been heaps of baking when I got to Mom's. Bread, fruit pastries, cookies.

I put out the nice china dishes. Wendy prepares Chamomile tea with honey.

"Maybe you could look for the passport after tea?" Mom says, taking a forkful of pie and lifting it shakily to her mouth.

"Sure," I say.

"She wants to travel," Wendy says to me. "She always wants to travel." She laughs slightly as she eats her pie. I don't like that. I don't like her making fun of Mom and talking about her as if she isn't right there.

"I'll go check on that passport, Mom," I say. "I'll be right back."

I walk to the closet in the hallway, hoping she hasn't moved it to another secret location. I feel around for the big blue box in the back of the closet. It is there. I open it and look in the dark leather folder. I gasp. The passport isn't there. I look more closely. Whew—there it is, hidden underneath all that dark blue. I walk back toward the kitchen, greatly relieved. All along the hallway, I stop to look at all the needlepoint those hands of hers have done throughout the years. What happens to all that talent, all those gifts?

Mom is back in the family room, ready for a rest. I sit down beside her, take her hand in mine, and gently massage the palm of her hand, her fingers. First one hand, then the other. I think of all the places she has been and all the work she has done and all the love she has given.

I look at her and smile. She smiles back.

"Did you find the passport?" she asks.

"I did. It's right where you left it. And now I've got to get going," I say, giving her a hug.

"And what about the tour?" she says. "How will they know where to pick me up?"

"You don't need to worry, Mom," I say. "I've cancelled it."

"Okay. That's probably for the best."

She looks at Wendy and says, "Will you take care of me?"

My eyes tear up as I walk out the door.

THE NIGHT SHE SLIPPED AWAY

I drive up the cedar tree-lined driveway. Slowly. Suspended in time. The dark asphalt glistens with frost. The headlights guide me to the top of the driveway. Once there, I sit for a moment, my head on the steering wheel, glancing up at the giant cedars, standing as if on guard, watching over the house and my mother in it.

I open the driver's door and get out. Take a deep breath and walk into the house. The laboured breathing has stopped. It is silent. So very silent.

For the past ten days, we have sat vigil. One by one, we came to sit and read with her, from Psalm 23: *"Der Herr ist mein Hirte, mir wird nichts mangeln"*—"The Lord is my Shepherd, I shall not want." The Christmas story from Luke, Chapter 2: *"Es begab sich aber zu der Zeit"*—"In those days a decree went out from Caesar Augustus that all the world should be enrolled..."

Her room is warm and safe, filled with love as she breathes in and out.

"Her heart is strong," the doctor says. "Just keep her comfortable."

The wood snaps and crackles in the fireplace. Ahhhh. Music, jazz and soul fill the air. I hear my daughter's voice belting out *"My Man"* from the stereo, followed by the peaceful and joyous sounds of German Christmas carols, sung a capella in glorious harmony. *"Es ist ein Ros Entsprungen," "Stille Nacht."* All is calm, all is bright.

I walk into Mom's room and wave "hi." She raises her

right hand. She is old now, ninety-one years today. But she does not look old. Her skin is smooth and hydrated. I reach for her hand and hold it. I lie down beside her and tell her, "Everyone is all right. The kids are all right. No need to worry. Everyone and everything is taken care of. Just rest." I feel her body relax.

A few of us have gathered to celebrate her birthday. She has never liked much attention, but she loves us, her family, with abandon.

I leave the bedroom and go into the kitchen to prepare coffee for everyone. We sit around the kitchen table, custom-made from cherry wood, the table around which we've heard and told so many stories; the table around which my brothers and I have started composing our mother's eulogy. We talk and laugh to mask the monumental void that is about to befall us. Suspended.

"Let's go in to see Mom," I say.

We head down the long hallway to the master bedroom and gather around her. We sing "Happy Birthday."

There is so much love in the room, so much warmth, as we accompany her on her journey.

Someone mentions songs for her memorial service. I want to yell "Stop! She is still with us. She can hear us." But I don't.

Her brow furrows. Is she in pain or overcome with emotion? She does not like to be seen like this, helpless and vulnerable with all eyes on her. She is the pillar of strength, the matriarch.

Once the guests are gone, she relaxes and her breath becomes even and steady once more. She falls into a sound sleep.

A few days later, while I am sitting with her, Stuart,

her youngest grandson, comes to visit.

"Hi Oma," he calls out as he enters the room. He radiates light and energy as he tells her of his upcoming trip to Hawaii and Hong Kong and China. She smiles, her eyes relaxing as he holds her hand, as if warmth is flooding her aging body. She squeezes his hand in return. Her eyes open for a few moments as she takes him in.

Later, the young Filipina caregiver, Mary Jane, sits on the bed with her, lies down beside her, sings to her, rubs her face with cream, and massages her hands, then her feet, with so much care and love. My mother falls into a deep sleep, her heartbeat strong and steady. And so it goes for days until one day, her laboured breathing becomes unbearable to hear. It is as though the cedar walls surrounding her expand and contract with each breath until finally they can no longer contain her. She exhales one last time and it is quiet, so very quiet.

Mary Jane calls to let us know that she is gone and I picture her, amidst her tears, going about her work, gathering dentures from their case in the bathroom, putting them in place, supporting the cooling neck with a towel, covering my mother's body. She is sitting vigil on the blue velvet chair in the corner, watching over Mom, when we arrive.

And so, one by one, we sit with her again to kiss her forehead now grown cold; to wish her a good journey, a safe crossing.

The woods are calm and quiet. It is a bitterly cold night, the night she slips away.

Acknowledgements

Most of these stories began during writing workshops led by Barbara Turner-Vesselago in Spain, Portugal, and different parts of Canada—it is interesting to see what comes up when one is removed from home, these stories that are waiting to be told.

Thank you to Louise Bergen Price, our family historian, who generously shared our family story in even more detail than that which I had heard from my mother. Thank you to my dear friends, who were kind enough to read various iterations of these stories and provide invaluable feedback. And to my daughter, Steph, who allowed me to share her birth story and who provided the title of this story collection.

The biggest thank you goes to my parents, who provided a safe and loving home in the country, in which to raise us. In the words of my father: "Every aspect of life can be seen, right here, on the farm."

About Atmosphere Press

Founded in 2015, Atmosphere Press was built on the principles of Honesty, Transparency, Professionalism, Kindness, and Making Your Book Awesome. As an ethical and author-friendly hybrid press, we stay true to that founding mission today.

If you're a reader, enter our giveaway for a free book here:

SCAN TO ENTER
BOOK GIVEAWAY

If you're a writer, submit your manuscript for consideration here:

SCAN TO SUBMIT
MANUSCRIPT

And always feel free to visit Atmosphere Press and our authors online at atmospherepress.com. See you there soon!

ABOUT THE AUTHOR

BETTY R WALL was born in British Columbia, Canada, to Russian Mennonite immigrants. From a young age, Betty has had a love of language and the written word, which ultimately led her to pursue a degree in Germanic Languages and Literatures at the University of Toronto. For most of her professional career, she has operated a translation and interpretation agency. In her free time, she continues to pursue her love of writing and travel, which has taken her to various parts of Europe, Africa, Asia and South America. She is the author of *No Way Out,* a Canada Book Awards Winner, published in 2021. *All That This House Has To Offer* is her first short story collection.

Visit bettyrwall.com.